The Riddle of the World

The Riddle of the World

A Reconsideration of Schopenhauer's Philosophy

Barbara Hannan

OXFORD
UNIVERSITY PRESS
2009

uᒉ
OXFORD
UNIVERSITY PRESS

Oxford University Press, Inc., publishes works that further
Oxford University's objective of excellence
in research, scholarship, and education.

Oxford   New York
Auckland   Cape Town   Dar es Salaam   Hong Kong   Karachi
Kuala Lumpur   Madrid   Melbourne   Mexico City   Nairobi
New Delhi   Shanghai   Taipei   Toronto

With offices in
Argentina   Austria   Brazil   Chile   Czech Republic   France   Greece
Guatemala   Hungary   Italy   Japan   Poland   Portugal   Singapore
South Korea   Switzerland   Thailand   Turkey   Ukraine   Vietnam

Published by Oxford University Press, Inc.
198 Madison Avenue, New York, New York 10016

www.oup.com

Oxford is a registered trademark of Oxford University Press.

Library of Congress Cataloging-in-Publication Data
Hannan, Barbara.
The riddle of the world : a reconsideration of Schopenhauer's
philosophy / Barbara Hannan.
    p. cm.
Includes bibliographical references.
ISBN 978-0-19-537894-8; 978-0-19-537893-1 (pbk.)
1. Schopenhauer, Arthur, 1788–1860.   I. Title.
B3148.H36 2009
193—dc22   2008041061

9 8 7 6 5 4 3 2 1

Printed in the United States of America
on acid-free paper

For my parents,
William S. Hannan and Nancy B. Hannan,
with all my love and gratitude.

[A]nything true that a man conceives, and anything obscure that he elucidates, will at some time or other be grasped by another thinking mind, and impress, delight, and console it. To such a man we speak, just as those like us have spoken to us, and have been our consolation in this wilderness of life.

—Arthur Schopenhauer, *The World as Will and Representation*

Wovon man nicht sprechen kann, darüber muss man schweigen.

(*What we cannot speak about must be consigned to silence.*)

—Ludwig Wittgenstein, *Tractatus Logico-Philosophicus*

PREFACE

This book is an introduction to the philosophy of Arthur Schopenhauer, written in a personal style. I aim to connect Schopenhauer's ideas with ongoing debates in philosophy and to invite readers to tackle Schopenhauer's work on their own. Another aim is to increase general appreciation of Schopenhauer's subliminal influence on other much-studied thinkers. For example, I see many scholars nowadays working on Wittgenstein. While these scholars may be dimly aware that Schopenhauer was an influence on their subject, most of them seem never to have actually *read* Schopenhauer. Schopenhauer is also insufficiently appreciated as one of the fathers of psychoanalysis and existentialism. To some extent, I would like to remedy this situation and get Schopenhauer more of the credit he deserves.

Schopenhauer speaks to me primarily because my personality is similar in many respects to his. Schopenhauer was an introvert who loved animals more than he loved people. So am I. He loved and respected empirical science (while appreciating its limitations), hated empty verbiage and intellectual pretension, and cared above all about the pursuit of truth. I do as well. He was pessimistic. So am I.

I agree with Schopenhauer that personality, rather than reasoning, is the primary source of philosophical views. In the ways my personality resembles Schopenhauer's, my philosophical instincts resemble his, too. I am constitutionally inclined to see the world much the same way Schopenhauer did. When I began to read

Schopenhauer seriously, I had the delightful experience of finding many of my own thoughts and conclusions expressed by one of the great philosophers of the past.[1] Schopenhauer's animism or panpsychism (his intuitive conviction that the inner nature of all things is the active mental force we experience in ourselves as *will*) appeals to me, as does his thesis that the metaphysical basis of ethics is empathy rather than reason. I am also irresistibly drawn to his idea that works of art, particularly music, somehow reveal truth—the way things are in themselves, behind the appearances. Schopenhauer's pessimism also appeals to my temperament.

The feature of Schopenhauer's thought that *least* appeals to me is his quasi-Kantian transcendental idealism. I reject pure anti-realism as incoherent: anti-realism about something, x, necessarily presupposes realism about something else, y. Schopenhauer saw himself as purifying Kant's transcendental idealism by returning it to the purer form defended by Berkeley. According to Berkeley, ordinary physical objects are unreal, but minds and their ideas are real. I believe that both Kant and Schopenhauer (not to mention Berkeley) would have been better off accepting ordinary physical objects as real (mind-independent). Fortunately, there are many elements in Schopenhauer's thought that pull in this commonsense direction.

One central thesis of this book is that Schopenhauer was half-consciously struggling to break with Kant and idealism altogether. The parts of Schopenhauer's philosophy with the most enduring value are the ones contrary to Kant. Schopenhauer's epistemology is simultaneously more empiricist and more rationalist than Kant's. His metaphysical ideas concerning the nature of the thing-in-itself

---

1. I should mention that my initial impression of Schopenhauer was not so positive. Many years ago when I was an undergraduate at Randolph-Macon Woman's College, I was introduced to Schopenhauer by reading his notorious essay "On Women." That essay is a revolting misogynist diatribe, entirely unworthy of Schopenhauer. Reading it turned me off to such an extent that I did not try to read anything by Schopenhauer again for twenty years. I am glad I eventually read his more respectable work. Still, his unjustified contempt for women remains a problem. Rudiger Safranski, author of a fine biography of Schopenhauer, may have discovered the real cause of Schopenhauer's misogyny—the bitterness of a rejected lover. Over and over again, Schopenhauer fell in love with women who did not want him. "As for women," Schopenhauer admitted late in life, "I was very fond of them, if only they would have had me." See Safranski, *Schopenhauer and the Wild Years of Philosophy*, trans. Ewald Osers (Cambridge: Harvard University Press, 1987), pp. 66–67.

undermine transcendental idealism. He gives a thorough and devastating critique of Kantian ethics.

Schopenhauer instructed his future readers to read everything he wrote, and to read it *twice*, in order to grasp the "single thought" at the heart of his philosophical system.[2] These days, few people have the patience or the luxury of time. Having the privilege of being a tenured professor, I have done as Schopenhauer instructed. This book contains a great deal of exposition of Schopenhauer's ideas and arguments. Some readers may find this tedious, asking, "Why should I read Hannan's book, when I could just read Schopenhauer himself?" Fair enough, but I believe there is value in what I have done in the expository sections, namely, to draw together in a concise and readable way the central thoughts of a great philosopher whose work has been unjustly neglected of late. There is some merit in being a *faithful* expositor. Anyone who reads this book will get a fair idea of what Schopenhauer really said, along with my criticisms and my own ideas.

During the years of working on this book, I have been engaged in a long conversation with Schopenhauer, a long-dead kindred spirit who still speaks to me through his work. This conversation has been a privilege and an education. Through clarifying in my own mind what Schopenhauer thought, along with where and why I agree and disagree with it, I have come to know myself and the world better. My hope is that others will find that Schopenhauer speaks for them as he does for me.

2. See *The World as Will and Representation*, trans. E. F. J. Payne, vol. 1 (New York: Dover, 1969), preface to the first edition.

ACKNOWLEDGMENTS

I owe an enormous debt to John Heil, who served as a reader of my manuscript for Oxford University Press. Heil read my work with sympathy, but also with critical rigor. He offered many thoughtful and insightful suggestions for revisions and improvements. I took all of his suggestions to heart, and the book is much better for it. Ted Honderich also reviewed the manuscript for Oxford. I thank him, too, for his many valuable comments and suggestions. I am especially grateful to Ted because of the following: several years ago, when I was just beginning to work on Schopenhauer, Ted heard me read a paper on Schopenhauer's views on the free will problem at a conference. He saw merit in the paper and posted it on his Determinism and Freedom Philosophy website. This bit of positive reinforcement came at a time when I was feeling discouraged and gave me the heart to go on and write this book.

Peter Ohlin, philosophy editor at Oxford University Press, has been helpful and supportive of the project from the beginning. Trish Watson, copy editor at Oxford, did a thorough and meticulous job on my manuscript and has my warmest thanks.

My sister, Elizabeth Hannan Cree, volunteered to help me with the index. (How convenient it is to have a sister who is a professional editor!) I am grateful for her assistance, as well as for her constant personal support.

Abraham "Brom" Anderson, a former colleague at the University of New Mexico, taught me much about Descartes and Spinoza, and thereby contributed to chapter 2. Conversations with Brom were instrumental in my development of the reading of the ontological argument defended in the same chapter.

Robert Watson wrote a beautiful MA thesis at the University of New Mexico a few years ago, using Schopenhauer's metaphysics as grounding for an environmental ethic. While I was on Robert's thesis committee, we had many conversations that eventually contributed to this book. Robert also sent me a copy of Schopenhauer's *On the Will in Nature* from France, at a time when I was having trouble obtaining a copy in the United States.

Mark Ralkowski, another talented graduate student at the University of New Mexico, read an early draft of chapter 3 and offered comments, convincing me to make substantial changes in that chapter. Those changes improved the chapter, and I am grateful.

George Patsakos, Professor of Physics Emeritus at the University of Idaho, has been my best friend since I met him almost twenty years ago. Without his constant support and encouragement, I doubt I would ever have written this book. I am also grateful to George in a more specific capacity—his expertise contributed to my discussion, in chapter 2, of quantum indeterminacy and its possible impact on the free will problem.

Finally, I thank two musicians (however strange it may seem to thank musicians for help with a philosophy book). Roger Melone is director of the New Mexico Symphony Orchestra Chorus. Michael Cooke is director of Quintessence, Choral Artists of the Southwest. Singing with these fine groups has given me whatever insight I possess into the nature of music and thus contributed greatly to chapter 4. It has also brought sufficient joy into my life to make me doubt my own pessimism. Thanks, Roger and Michael—you helped me find my voice, in more ways than one.

CONTENTS

The Riddle of the World

CHAPTER ONE

A Sketch of Schopenhauer's Central Ideas

A Neglected Genius

Arthur Schopenhauer was much annoyed by the fact that his philosophy was insufficiently appreciated within his own lifetime. He took this annoying fact as evidence, however, that he was a true genius, since a genius's contemporaries never understand him. The genius must await understanding by future minds.

Schopenhauer was egotistical, but his pompous pronouncements about himself were not altogether wrong. He *was* a genius. His works sank into the collective unconscious of the next generation of thinkers.[1] That next generation included Nietzsche, Freud, Jung, and Wittgenstein. Too often, Schopenhauer's ideas appear in the works of these major figures without their true author being openly acknowledged.

The enduring value of Schopenhauer's philosophy lies not in its being the one true metaphysics (there can be no such thing),

---

1. I use the term "collective unconscious" with the odd sense that I am applying one of Schopenhauer's own concepts to my account of the fate of Schopenhauer's theories. Jung's idea of the collective unconscious was almost certainly suggested to him by Schopenhauer's idea of the Will (unconscious, prerational mind) as thing-in-itself. Jung (unlike Freud) openly acknowledged that he had read, and been deeply influenced by, Schopenhauer. See Anthony Storr, introduction to *The Essential Jung* (Princeton: Princeton University Press, 1983).

but rather in its suggesting various hypotheses that *might* be true. Twentieth-century philosophy of science has taught us that there is no clear demarcation between science and metaphysics. Schopenhauer's brilliant speculations cannot simply be dismissed as unscientific. While some of his hypotheses have proven false,[2] others remain contenders for our serious attention.

In this chapter, I do my best to lay out Schopenhauer's most important philosophical ideas without being overly critical.

The Fourfold Root

The great paradox of Schopenhauer is that he is a transcendental idealist, yet he thinks we can know the nature of the thing-in-itself. For the time being, let us leave aside the thing-in-itself and confine ourselves to the realm of phenomena. Within this empirical world, the realm of cognition, everything has an explanation, according to Schopenhauer. There are four types of explanation, each a different version of the Principle of Sufficient Reason. This is the thesis of Schopenhauer's first book, which served as his doctoral dissertation, *On the Fourfold Root of the Principle of Sufficient Reason*. Schopenhauer never officially changed his mind about any of the theses defended in this book, and he considered it to be an essential preface to everything else he ever wrote. Schopenhauer formulates the Principle of Sufficient Reason in these terms: "Nothing is without a ground or reason why it is."[3] Each of the four types of explanation corresponds to a type of object-for-the-human-understanding.

Before we survey the four types of explanation and their corresponding objects, it is important to grasp Schopenhauer's account of the structure of the human cognitive faculty. In human beings, the cognitive faculty consists of two subfaculties, understanding

2. E.g., Schopenhauer believed that a person's character shows in his or her physiognomy. A handsome, well-shaped head indicates good character, whereas a misshapen, unattractive head indicates character flaws. There are numerous counter-examples to this. If Schopenhauer were correct, Alcibiades would have been a better man than Socrates. Schopenhauer also expressed the odd view (now clearly falsified) that character is inherited from the father, and intellect from the mother. I do not mention here Schopenhauer's numerous mistaken, and clearly falsified, views regarding the nature of women.

3. Schopenhauer, *On the Fourfold Root of the Principle of Sufficient Reason*, trans. E. F. J. Payne (La Salle, Ill.: Open Court Publishing, 1974), p. 6.

[*Verstand*] and reason [*Vernunft*]. Understanding is a faculty we share with nonhuman animals. Only human beings possess reason. Understanding is the faculty that organizes experience according to time, space, and causality. Reason is the "higher" faculty of abstract concepts and language. Reason divides objects into classes and names these classes. Because human beings possess reason in addition to understanding, we are capable of ascending to the meta-level and seeing that space, time, and causality are forms imposed on reality by the mind. We can then contemplate these forms themselves as objects of thought. We are also capable of contemplating classes of object (types, properties) as complex objects of thought. Accordingly, there are more kinds of objects-for-the-understanding in human beings than in nonhuman animals.

I cannot resist a slight digression at this point. One of the charming features of Schopenhauer's philosophy is his appreciation of the intelligence of nonhuman animals:

> All animals, even the lowest, must have understanding, that is to say, knowledge of the law of causality, although they may have it in very different degrees of keenness and clearness. At any rate they must always have as much as is necessary for intuitive perception with their senses; for sensation without understanding would be not merely a useless, but even a cruel, gift of nature. No one who himself has any intelligence will doubt its existence in the higher animals.[4]

I must say, I cannot agree more. I have long been baffled by the number of respected philosophers who hold, in absurd contradiction to plain evidence, that nonhuman animals don't think,[5] or don't live in the world,[6] or don't divide reality into particulars,[7] because of their lack of language. Schopenhauer sees the truth, that division of the world into spatiotemporal particulars and appreciation of cause–effect relationships are basic cognitive abilities that are prior to linguistic thought. Why so many reputedly great philosophers have missed this point is a mystery to me.

4. Schopenhauer, *Fourfold Root*, p. 110.

5. See Donald Davidson, "Thought and Talk," in *Inquiries into Truth and Interpretation* (Oxford: Clarendon Press, 1984), pp. 155–170.

6. See John McDowell, *Mind and World* (Cambridge: Harvard University Press, 1994), chap. 6, pp. 108–126.

7. See Wilfrid Sellars, *Empiricism and the Philosophy of Mind* (Cambridge: Harvard University Press, 1997), p. 63.

To return to our main topic, Schopenhauer says the four types of explanation are as follows:

1. Causal explanations of the familiar scientific sort
2. Logical (propositional) inferences
3. Geometrical or mathematical inferences
4. Explanations of action making reference to motives

Schopenhauer is careful to point out that category 4 represents a special class of causal explanation: "Motivation is causality seen from within."[8]

The four types of object-for-the-human-understanding, corresponding to the four types of explanation and listed in order, are

1. Physical objects
2. Concepts [types, properties, classes]
3. Space and time, contemplated as the forms of inner and outer sense
4. The subject of willing known uniquely to each individual via self-consciousness

Schopenhauer insists that causes and effects are changes or events, not entities or things. Causes and effects are changes in a subject that necessarily exists eternally and prior to these changes. The notion of a "first cause" is absurd—every cause necessarily presupposes a preceding cause, and so on infinitely. A further point is stressed in various places in Schopenhauer's writings: causal explanations always leave something unexplained. These explanations terminate in appeal to natural forces, which are irreducible features of the necessarily existing subject of causal relations: "Every causality and every explanation presupposes some original force; therefore an explanation never explains everything, but always leaves something inexplicable. We see this in the whole of physics and chemistry."[9]

As an example of a natural force, we could mention electricity. According to Schopenhauer, natural forces do not cause anything. For example, to say, "The lamp was caused to come on by electricity" is misleading. In truth, the lamp was caused to come on by some change or event, and all changes and events take place against a background of inexplicable natural forces.

8. Schopenhauer, *Fourfold Root*, p. 214.
9. Schopenhauer, *Prize Essay on the Freedom of the Will*, trans. E. F. J. Payne, ed. Gunter Zoller (Cambridge: Cambridge University Press, 1999), p. 41.

Schopenhauer's views on causation are rather confusing and not altogether satisfactory. He says that the basic forces of nature include not just electromagnetism and gravity, but natural *kinds* such as chemical kinds (elements) and vegetable and animal species. This is Schopenhauer's doctrine of the "Platonic Forms," about which I will have more to say later. He observes that basic forces of nature, including natural kinds, are that which "first gives to causes their causality, i.e., the ability to act, and hence that by which the causes hold this ability merely in fee."[10] Thus, Schopenhauer seems to believe (though he does not openly acknowledge it) that there are two kinds of cause, which we might call (following Fred Dretske) "triggering causes" and "structuring causes."[11] As Dretske puts it, specifying the triggering cause explains why x happens *now*; specifying the structuring cause explains why x happens as opposed to y. For Schopenhauer, changes or events are triggering causes, whereas the basic forces of nature, including the character or structure of chemical, vegetable, and animal kinds, are structuring causes.

Schopenhauer does not believe that the vital force, that which moves living organisms to respond to stimuli and to act voluntarily, is reducible to other, more basic natural forces. The vital force, further differentiated into the character of each plant and animal species and the individual character of each human being, is ontologically distinct from chemical and physical forces. As a consequence, the type of causal explanation making reference to stimuli or motives terminates in appeal to the vital force, just as the type of causal explanation making reference to physical causes terminates in appeal to electromagnetism, gravity, and so forth.[12]

---

10. Schopenhauer, *Fourfold Root*, p. 67.

11. Fred Dretske, *Explaining Behavior: Reasons in a World of Causes* (Cambridge: MIT Press, 1988), p. 42. Dretske describes structuring causes in terms of events. I think he should have said that structuring causes may be, and typically are, substances. In general, my treatment of causation in this book may strike some readers as superficial. I have chosen not to go into the details of philosophical analysis of the concept of causation, relying on the reader's intuitive sense that to *cause* x is to *make x happen*. Readers who wish to investigate causality more thoroughly would be well advised to begin with the first chapter of Ted Honderich's *How Free Are You? The Determinism Problem* (Oxford: Oxford University Press, 1993). The next step might be to look at a fine collection of papers, *Causation*, ed. Ernest Sosa and Michael Tooley (Oxford: Oxford University Press, 1993).

12. See Schopenhauer, *The World as Will and Representation* (hereafter *WWR*), trans. E. F. J. Payne (New York: Dover, 1969), vol. 1, p. 142.

Schopenhauer's use of the term "vital force" is unfortunate, since it carries connotations of scientific views no longer respectable. Everyone knows nowadays that organisms contain no "animal spirits" or *élan vital*, or whatever you might want to call it—no special stuff that makes them alive. Organisms are made of the same stuff as everything else. When we investigate the construction and operation of living things, all we find are chemicals and electricity. It still remains true, however, that living things possess properties (metabolism, self-replication, self-repair, etc.) that we cannot currently explain on the basis of the properties of nonliving matter. The most generous way to understand Schopenhauer, when he says there is a vital force, is as endorsing emergentism rather than reductionism. He believes that different sorts of property or causal power appear at different ontological levels. Hence, he predicts, we will never be able to reduce biology to chemistry.

It is rather curious that many modern biologists seem happy enough to endorse emergentism but would not be caught dead endorsing vitalism. "Vitalism" has become a dirty word. This is curious because emergentism *is* a sort of vitalism. We might call it "property vitalism" as opposed to "substance vitalism," on analogy with dualism in philosophy of mind. At any rate, emergentism with regard to the properties of living systems certainly pulls in the direction of vitalism, though few modern thinkers seem to realize this.[13] Since emergentism is still a live option, we may conclude that Schopenhauer's vitalism is not so quaint and outmoded as it might at first seem.

Transcendental Idealism and the Metaphysics of Will

Though Schopenhauer did not by any means agree with all of Kant's philosophy, he found an epiphany in Kantian transcendental idealism. He quotes Rousseau in this regard: "Quit thy childhood, my friend, and wake up."[14] For Schopenhauer, the naive realism

---

13. One thinker who does realize this is Jaegwon Kim. See his paper "The Non-reductivists' Troubles with Mental Causation," in John Heil and Alfred Mele, eds., *Mental Causation* (Oxford: Oxford University Press, 1993), pp. 189–210. See especially pp. 198–200.

14. This quotation from Rousseau is the motto appearing at the beginning of *WWR*, vol. 1, bk. 1.

presupposed by Western science is a childish error. One breaks the spell of that error, and enters intellectual adulthood, only when one realizes that the empirical world is as much a construction of the mind as it is an objective reality. Object and subject presuppose one another.

The scientific mind protests against idealism by saying, "Surely there was a world, and a greater universe, before living creatures evolved to behold it. Mind is a creation of matter, not vice versa." But Schopenhauer points out that even if we agree with this, Berkeley's argument[15] remains vexingly irrefutable: when we imagine the world existing prior to the evolution of minds, we are covertly presupposing a subject apprehending and categorizing that world.

Schopenhauer calls this (the equal irrefutability of both scientific naturalism and Berkelean idealism) "an antinomy in our faculty of knowledge." The passage in which Schopenhauer describes this antinomy is memorable:

> Suns and planets with no eye to see them and no understanding to know them can of course be spoken of in words, but...these words are [an absurdity], an "iron-wood."...[T]he law of causality, and the consideration and investigation of nature which follow on it, lead us necessarily to the certain assumption that each more highly organized state of matter succeeded in time a cruder state. Thus animals existed before men, fishes before land animals, plants before fishes, and the inorganic before that which is organic; consequently the original mass had to go through a long series of changes before the first eye could be opened. And yet the existence of this whole world remains for ever dependent on that first eye that opened, were it even that of an insect. For such an eye necessarily brings about knowledge, for which and in which alone the whole world is, and without which it is not even conceivable. The world is entirely representation, and as such requires the knowing subject as the supporter of its existence. That long course of time itself, filled with innumerable changes, through which matter rose from form to form, till finally there came into existence the first knowing animal, the whole of this time itself is alone thinkable in the identity of a consciousness. This world is the succession of the representations of this consciousness, the form of its knowing, and apart from this loses all meaning, and is nothing at all. Thus we see, on the one hand, the existence of

15. See Berkeley, *Principles of Human Knowledge*, pt. 1, secs. 3, 6, 22–24.

the whole world necessarily dependent on the first knowing being, however imperfect it be; on the other hand, this first knowing animal just as necessarily wholly dependent on a long chain of causes and effects which has preceded it, and in which it itself appears as a small link. These two contradictory views, to each of which we are led with equal necessity, might certainly be called an *antinomy* in our faculty of knowledge.[16]

The only way out of the contradiction, according to Schopenhauer, is to embrace a modified version of Kantian transcendental idealism.[17] Time, space, and causality are forms of appearance; they belong only to phenomena, not to things-in-themselves. It is not easy to see how adopting transcendental idealism makes the problem go away.

Another set of problems leaps glaringly out at this point. Schopenhauer (rightly, I believe) insists that nonhuman animals can think; they possess understanding if not reason. Yet, when Schopenhauer endorses idealism, he implies that nonhuman animals are mere constructs in the minds of human beings. No, wait—even an insect can be the creator and supporter of a world, before human beings evolve. Presumably, an insect's world lacks all the intricacies of the world-for-human-beings. But then, wouldn't the world-for-human-beings have to exist in order for something like an insect (with all its intricacies) to exist at all? There are inconsistencies in Schopenhauer's thought here I cannot resolve.

Anyway, how is transcendental idealism supposed to remove the alleged antinomy in our faculty of thought? The best I can do, attempting to express Schopenhauer's evident reasoning, is this: transcendental idealism enables us to see that scientific materialism and philosophical idealism operate at two different levels, so there is really no contradiction between them. Scientific materialism and the evolutionary theory to which it leads[18] are fine, as far as they go. But they do not go beyond their own level, the level of describing the empirical world, the world as human inquirers must come to understand it. There is another level, a metaphysical level, a level at which we can intuit how things are in themselves. Philosophy, as

---

16. *WWR*, vol. 1, p. 30.

17. Schopenhauer's epistemology departs in many respects from Kant's. For Schopenhauer's full critique of Kant, see *WWR*, vol. 1, appendix.

18. Note that while Charles Darwin may have read Schopenhauer, Schopenhauer could not possibly have been influenced by Darwin. *The Origin of Species* was published in 1859; Schopenhauer died in 1861.

opposed to science, occurs at this other level. This is difficult to reconcile with Schopenhauer's assertion that the source of metaphysical knowledge is "inner and outer experience,"[19] the same as the source of empirical scientific knowledge. I do not attempt to reconcile this tension here, but I have more to say in chapter 2 about the internal conflicts in Schopenhauer's philosophy that undermine his transcendental idealism.

Let us return to the Berkelean argument on which Schopenhauer relies in stating his antinomy: we cannot really imagine a world existing independently of a conceiving mind; when we think we can, we are fooling ourselves, because the subject is unavoidably presupposed by the positing of objects. Berkeley's argument may be reconstructed as follows: imagine, say, an asteroid orbiting outside the light cone of a conscious creature. Are you imagining an unperceived object? Or (Berkeley's point) are you imagining how such an asteroid would look, feel, and so on? If the latter, you have not really eliminated the perceiver.

This argument, it may be said, commits a fallacy—it conflates *the act of imagining* a world without consciousness with *the object* of that act (with what is imagined). It may be true that the act of imagining requires a subject, but does it follow that there must be a subject present in the world thereby imagined? Not obviously. Ultimately, I must conclude that Berkeley and other idealists are guilty of some kind of incoherence, if not exactly this alleged fallacy. However, I put off a complete discussion of this matter until chapter 2.

Returning to exposition, Schopenhauer thinks that materialism is *scientifically* adequate, but a *philosophical* dead end. Materialism "carries death in its heart even at its birth."[20] Schopenhauer identifies Plato and Kant (idealists both, though idealists of very different kinds) as the deepest thinkers in the history of Western philosophy. What Plato and Kant have in common, the feature Schopenhauer seizes upon as deeply significant, is this: they agree that the space-time world, the world of empirical experience, is not quite real; what's really real is beyond it, beyond science, beyond empirical knowledge. As Plato put it, the world of observation, the world of particulars in space and time, is always *becoming* but never *is*. It is a mere unreal shadow of true reality (the eternal, unchanging Forms).

19. *WWR*, vol. 1, appendix, p. 428.
20. *WWR*, vol. 1, p. 29.

As Kant put it, the thing-in-itself is a necessary presupposition of knowledge, but it itself can never be known. What we can know, the objects of experience, are constructs of our minds (though they incorporate "intuitions" emanating from whatever is out there). What Plato and Kant seem not to share is their view about types (classes, properties, kinds). Whereas Plato thinks ultimate reality really is individuated into types (Forms), Kant evidently denies this. For Kant, classification of reality into types takes place only when the mind intervenes; we impose types on reality. While Schopenhauer officially sides with Kant, he seems irresistibly drawn in the opposite direction at the same time. With his doctrine of the different grades of the Will's objectification,[21] Schopenhauer seems almost to acknowledge that these grades (natural kinds) are really *out there*, independent of human cognition. This is Schopenhauer's doctrine of the Platonic Forms, and it requires some explanation.

In addition to maintaining that the thing-in-itself is Will, Schopenhauer asserts that the Will "objectifies itself" in certain determinate "grades" or "levels." These are the Ideas or Platonic Forms. Each natural force (electromagnetism, gravity, chemical affinities, the vital force peculiar to living beings) and each natural kind (the character of each plant and animal species, and the unique character of each individual human being) is identical with one of these Ideas. How there could be such Ideas is difficult to grasp, since the thing-in-itself is supposed to be nonindividuated (the principle of individuation belongs to cognition and therefore applies only to objects in the phenomenal world). When Schopenhauer asserts that the thing-in-itself divides itself into distinct natural forces and natural kinds, he seems to be asserting something inconsistent—that the thing-in-itself is both differentiated and undifferentiated.

Schopenhauer attempts to ameliorate the inconsistency by saying that the Ideas are not quite noumenal. They exhibit reality under a very basic cognitive form, the form of representation-in-general. They are the "most adequate objectivity" or "most direct mirror" of the Will. The subject "becomes no longer individual" insofar as the subject knows the Ideas, because the Ideas exhibit "the *real* world as

---

21. I follow the convention of spelling "Will" with a capital "W" when I mean the undifferentiated thing-in-itself, and spelling "will" with a lowercase "w" when I mean the will of an individual. Schopenhauer himself does not always consistently follow this convention.

representation" instead of the illusory world as representation that is split off into individuals and comprehended by means of the principle of sufficient reason.[22] Schopenhauer evidently struggles with the Ideas—he wants to say that they are real independently of human cognition, and yet that they are not quite as real as the undifferentiated Will.

Schopenhauer maintains that the genius achieves a state of "pure, will-less knowing" in which he sees the Platonic Ideas straight on and can thereafter communicate the nature of reality to his audience. (The genius is always an artist. The scientist, being confined to the individuated world of space-time particulars governed by the principle of sufficient reason, does not apprehend the Ideas.) In general, says Schopenhauer, the intellect (reason) is subordinate to will. Will is the original psychic faculty, out of which reason arises secondarily.[23] So, how is it possible for the intellect of the genius to achieve "will-less knowing"? It would seem that intellect cannot detach itself from the will! This is as mysterious as the ability of the Platonic Forms to separate themselves off from the great Will. These are contradictions in Schopenhauer for which I cannot account.

This primacy of will over intellect has another interesting dimension. Schopenhauer was aware that his major conclusions were the deliverance of intuition (which is the product of character or will) rather than intellect. He even acknowledges that we cannot expect intellect to be able to account for such conclusions fully and consistently. In the last book of volume 1 of *The World as Will and Representation* (hereafter *WWR*), he says that true metaphysical convictions show themselves in action or conduct and that it is a matter of indifference how reason chooses to support these convictions. Action or conduct, of course, proceeds from will. In one person, reason will look to Christian dogma for after-the-fact justification

22. See *WWR*, vol. 1, secs. 32–34 (pp. 174–181).

23. See, e.g., *WWR*, vol. 2, chap. 19 (p. 205): "[I]n all animal beings the *will* is the primary and substantial thing; the *intellect*, on the other hand, is something secondary and additional, in fact a mere tool in the service of the will." The reader may be reminded here of Freudian psychology, in which id is the basic psychic faculty, from which ego and superego arise. Thomas Mann reportedly observed that Freud's theories were Schopenhauer's doctrines translated from the language of metaphysics into that of psychology. See Frank J. Sulloway, *Freud: Biologist of the Mind* (Cambridge: Harvard University Press, 1992), p. 253. For the Freudian view, see Freud, *An Outline of Psycho-analysis*, trans. James Strachey (New York: W. W. Norton and Co., 1949).

of its views; in another, to Buddhist belief; in still another, to philosophical argument. But it is all the same in the end. The intuitive conviction (which arises out of the individual's will or character) is prior to, and ultimately unjustifiable by, the reasons advanced in its support.[24]

Schopenhauer is anti-materialist in two, curiously different ways. As we have seen, he is a transcendental idealist; he believes there can be no object without a subject. Schopenhauer is also opposed to materialistic *reductionism*, the idea that all natural kinds are ultimately physical kinds. This anti-reductionism is a consequence of Schopenhauer's strong attraction to the metaphysical reality of natural kinds. Note this striking argument against physicalistic reductionism:

> [W]e still find it stated that the aim of physiological explanation is the reduction of organic life to the universal forces considered by physics....Accordingly, heat and electricity would really be the thing-in-itself, and the animal and plant worlds its phenomenon....If we examine the matter closely, then ultimately at the basis of these views is the presupposition that the organism is only an aggregate of phenomena of physical, chemical, and mechanical forces that have come together in it by chance, and have brought about the organism as a freak of nature without further significance. Accordingly, the organism of an animal or of a human being would be, philosophically considered, not the exhibition of a particular Idea, in other worlds, not immediate objectivity of the Will at a definite higher grade, but there would appear in it only those Ideas that objectify Will in electricity, chemistry, and mechanism. Hence the organism would be just as fortuitously put together from the chance meeting of these forces as are the forms of men and animals in clouds or stalactites; and hence it itself it would be no more interesting.[25]

Here Schopenhauer implies that all natural kinds (physical, chemical, and biological) are objectifications of the thing-in-itself; thus, they are ontologically real. These types are not imposed on reality by the human mind; they are out there to be discovered. Further,

---

24. Here it is fairly obvious that Schopenhauer influenced both Wittgenstein and William James. See Wittgenstein, "Lecture on Ethics," in *Ludwig Wittgenstein: Philosophical Occasions 1912–1951*, ed. James Klagge and Alfred Nordmann (Indianapolis: Hackett, 1993), pp. 37–44; James, *The Varieties of Religious Experience* (New York: New American Library, 1958).

25. *WWR*, vol. I, p. 142.

higher types do not reduce to more fundamental types. It is fine with Schopenhauer if the different sciences remain autonomous with respect to one another; in fact, this is the way it should be, since it represents the fact that nature divides itself into kinds, and explanation stops when we reach the natural forces represented by those kinds.

In such passages, Schopenhauer appears to be thinking of natural kinds as something like Aristotelian substantial forms. There is an obvious conflict between such a view and transcendental idealism, according to which the thing-in-itself is an undifferentiated blob, carved up into kinds by human cognitive activity.

Schopenhauer's philosophy is filled with this kind of tension. While he officially insists that science operates only at the level of representation, his doctrine of the Platonic Forms clearly implies that science does investigate the thing-in-itself—after all, science classifies things into their natural kinds.

Should I try to resolve this tension and somehow reveal Schopenhauer's philosophy to be consistent? I cannot. Schopenhauer's philosophy is not consistent. Schopenhauer was a transitional thinker, bridging the gap between nineteenth-century and twentieth-century paradigms. It is typical of such transitional thinkers that they are officially working within a framework that they are also (half-consciously) trying to overturn. In Schopenhauer's case, he was both working within the Kantian paradigm of transcendental idealism and also half-consciously pushing toward a new epistemology in which both science and metaphysics, seamlessly blending into each other, both depend and do not depend on experience. It is not surprising that transitional thinkers contradict themselves, and perhaps we should not condemn them for doing so—provided we think they are struggling to tell us something important.

Let us return for a moment to Schopenhauer's citation of Kant and Plato as his two favorite philosophers. We were considering what Plato and Kant have in common, and what divides them. In addition to their difference over the ultimate reality of natural kinds, Plato and Kant seem to differ in their degree of epistemic optimism. Kant says that metaphysical knowledge (knowledge of ultimate reality or the thing-in-itself) is just flat-out impossible. All philosophy can do, according to Kant, is "critique," the activity of finding out the a priori conditions of knowledge. Plato, by contrast, seems to believe that a few people can actually know ultimate reality, at least to some extent—this is suggested by the allegory of the cave in Book VII of

Republic. Indeed, for Plato, in some sense we all know ultimate reality but have forgotten it, and the most intelligent or gifted souls are the ones who can be stimulated to remember. Schopenhauer, with his doctrine of the Ideas or grades of the Will's objectification, and with his notion that the artist of genius can know these Ideas, seems to be trying to recapture Plato's hopefulness.

Schopenhauer's cognitive psychology drastically simplifies Kant's scheme of categories, reducing all the categories to one (cause and effect). Or, perhaps I should say he relocates all the categories other than causation in the reason rather than the understanding. He also departs from Kant in declaring that the thing-in-itself is that which we know directly in ourselves as *will,* and which manifests itself in nonliving things as basic physical forces such as electromagnetism and gravity. Since the thesis that the thing-in-itself is Will is the centerpiece of Schopenhauer's philosophy, we must take a close look at how he arrives at this thesis.

To begin with, we must note that it is paradoxical to have a thesis about the thing-in-itself at all. Since the principle of individuation belongs to cognition, the noumenal realm contains no objects to be the referents of words, or even of thoughts. Therefore, it would seem that we cannot write about it or think about it. As Wittgenstein was to say in the last line of his *Tractatus,* "What we cannot speak about, we must pass over in silence."[26] Schopenhauer, however, thinks he *can* say something meaningful about the thing-in-itself—indeed, he can say quite a lot. This is because, according to Schopenhauer, we can learn about the nature of the thing-in-itself by looking at that which is *not* the thing-in-itself. The nature of the world as Will *shows* itself in the world as representation. Therefore, to do metaphysics, all we have to do is to *look* at the empirical world.

This fundamental idea, that the source of metaphysical truth is simply empirical observation (including introspection), is stated clearly in the appendix to volume 1 of *WWR,* in which Schopenhauer presents his criticism of the Kantian philosophy. Schopenhauer

---

26. Ludwig Wittgenstein, *Tractatus Logico-Philosophicus,* trans. D. F. Pears and B. F. McGuinness (London: Routledge, 1961), p. 74. The *Tractatus* is filled with images and ideas that obviously have their origin in Schopenhauer's work. See particularly 5.6–5.641 and 6.423–7. These images and ideas evidently took root in Wittgenstein's mind when he read *WWR* in his youth. See Ray Monk, *Ludwig Wittgenstein: The Duty of Genius* (London: Vintage, 1990), pp. 143–144; Allan Janik and Stephen Toulmin, *Wittgenstein's Vienna* (New York: Simon and Schuster, 1973).

attacks Kant for saying, in section 1 of the *Prolegomena*, that "the source of metaphysics cannot be empirical at all; its fundamental principles and concepts can never be taken from experience, either inner or outer." According to Schopenhauer, Kant never establishes this cardinal assertion, and Schopenhauer's own position about the source of metaphysics is quite contrary to Kant's:

> The world and our own existence present themselves to us necessarily as a riddle.... [Kant] assumed beforehand that metaphysics and knowledge *a priori* were identical; yet for this it would have been necessary first to demonstrate that the material for solving the riddle of the world cannot possibly be contained in the world itself, but is to be sought only outside it, in something we can reach only under the guidance of those forms of which we are *a priori* conscious. But so long as this is not proved, we have no ground for shutting ourselves off from the richest of all sources of knowledge, inner and outer experience.... Therefore, I say that the solution to the riddle of the world must come from an understanding of the world itself; and hence that the task of metaphysics is not to pass over experience in which the world exists, but to understand it thoroughly.... I say, therefore, that the solution to the riddle of the world is possible only through the proper connexion of outer with inner experience, carried out at the right point, and by the combination, thus effected, of these two very heterogeneous sources of knowledge. Yet this is so within certain limits inseparable from our finite nature, consequently so that we arrive at a correct understanding of the world itself without reaching an explanation of its existence which is conclusive and does away with all further problems.... [M]y path lies midway between the doctrine of omniscience of the earlier dogmatism and despair of the Kantian Critique.[27]

Here again, we glimpse an important, and little-appreciated, connection between Schopenhauer and Wittgenstein. Consider Schopenhauer's statement that "the solution to the riddle of the world is possible only through the proper connexion of outer with inner experience, carried out at the right point...by the *combination* thus effected." When Wittgenstein discusses "the riddle" in his *Tractatus*, he expresses the view that the fundamental problem of human existence cannot be posed in language, nor can its solution be put into words. If there is a solution to the riddle, it lies at least partly in a fundamental change in the *subject*, the self that constitutes

27. *WWR*, vol. 1, appendix, pp. 427–428.

the support and limit of the world.[28] This is a Schopenhauerian view. Schopenhauer's thought, indeed, is at the root of Wittgenstein's famous distinction between what can be *said* and what can only be *shown*. I say more about this in subsequent chapters. Returning to the main line of exposition: according to Schopenhauer, metaphysics consists in attempting to find the solution of "the riddle of the world," and the solution to that riddle (inconclusive and incomplete though it may be) is to be found at the intersection of inner and outer experience.

What is "the riddle of the world," anyway? I believe I know what Schopenhauer is talking about. I have spent my entire life feeling like a stranger in the world and asking myself, over and over, in countless different ways, "What is going on? What am I, and what am I doing here, and how do I fit into this madness I see all around me?" This existential bewilderment, just as Schopenhauer himself says, presents itself sometimes as the ethical problem (when I try to figure out how I should live), sometimes as the scientific or metaphysical problem (when I try to figure out what is real or true), and sometimes as the aesthetic problem (when nature, art, or music brings me comfort, and I wonder why).[29] But I am the admittedly unusual sort of person who is drawn to philosophy. Many people (maybe even most people), it seems, do not feel the riddle of the world at all. They conclude early on that life is about making money, or having a family, or becoming successful, and proceed to live in accordance with these conclusions, never questioning them. Or they accept the answers provided by religion, refusing to consider whether religion is really plausible. A person must have a certain level of intelligence, and a certain personality type, I believe, even to think there is a riddle of the world. Or perhaps I'm wrong. Maybe it's just that most people don't want to think about or talk about the riddle of the world, because it frightens them.

The riddle of the world is also the problem of evil. Why are suffering and death necessary? As Schopenhauer acutely notes, happiness is possible only as the temporary relief from some discomfort. We are driven psychologically to desire something metaphysically impossible—a state of perfect happiness and peace, undisturbed by suffering and strife. That, too, is the riddle of the world.

28. See Wittgenstein, *Tractatus*, 6.43, 6.5.

29. See the preface to the first edition of *WWR*, vol. 1, where Schopenhauer insists that his views on metaphysics, aesthetics, and ethics are three aspects of "a single thought."

But I digress. Let us focus on Schopenhauer's idea that metaphysical inquiry is a variety of empirical inquiry, and on his subsequent argument that the thing-in-itself is Will. The argument, interestingly, is nowhere spelled out in Schopenhauer's works in an orderly sequence of premises to conclusion. One must read everything Schopenhauer wrote in order to piece the argument together, though he comes closest to stating it clearly in the second book of the first volume of *WWR*.

Schopenhauer's argument begins with the observation that all causal explanations terminate in reference to natural forces. These natural forces have no explanation. They constitute an inexplicable background presupposed by the activity of causal explanation. As noted above, Schopenhauer agrees with Kant that space and time are the a priori forms of sensible intuition, but he simplifies Kant's scheme of categories of the understanding. For Schopenhauer, causality is the one and only category—the a priori schema making experience of a world possible. The faculty of understanding, shared by human beings and nonhuman animals, is the faculty that perceptually encounters causal connections. So, it is curious that causal explanations end in appeal to natural forces. It is as if we recognize, in our recognition of natural forces, that there is a noumenal realm—a reality that we cannot understand. When we confront the basic natural forces, we confront the thing-in-itself as directly as we are capable of doing.

Next, Schopenhauer asserts that motivation is causality seen from within. The fourth form of the principle of sufficient reason (the action of a living being necessarily results from the interplay of character with stimulus or motive) is really just a special case of the first form of the principle of sufficient reason (any change in the state of matter necessarily must have a cause).

It is impossible to overstate the importance of this second premise. As the assertion *cogito ergo sum* stands to the Cartesian philosophy, so the insight "we can see causality from within" stands to Schopenhauer's new edifice. In fact, it is useful to compare Descartes's reasoning to Schopenhauer's.

Descartes reasons roughly as follows: "I am something. But what am I? All of my ideas, including the idea of my body, could be illusions. But still, something must exist to think these illusions. Therefore, I am essentially a thinking thing."[30]

---

30. See Descartes, *Meditations*. Descartes's official doctrine is that the self is a *thing*, a *substance*, not a mode (not a mere way some substance is organized). A table, by contrast, is a mode, a way the extended substance is organized.

Schopenhauer's starting point is the same, but the subsequent reasoning is subtler and more complicated: "I am something. But what am I? All of my ideas, including the idea of my body, are constructions of the faculty of understanding, and so are as much illusion as they are reality. However, I have a relationship to the idea of my body that I bear to no other idea. Not only can I perceive my body from without, as a physical object in space and time, subject to cause and effect, like any other physical object, but I can cause my body to move through my own acts of will. Of course, any act of will that I perform is the necessary result of my character interacting with an external motive; but all such explanations of action (like causal explanations generally) terminate in reference to an inexplicable natural force. In the case of my own actions, this natural force is my character itself. I know my character in two ways: empirically, by observing my own actions over a lifetime, and directly, because I *am* my character. As such, as my directly known or intelligible character, I am one of the essential natural forces presupposed by all causal explanations. This intelligible character I recognize as (free) *will*. All of this suggests that if any other natural force were conscious of itself, it too would recognize itself as will."

The last line (the great conclusion that the in-itself of all phenomena is Will) does not follow logically from the premises. It is at best a suggestion based on analogy. Even the previous move (the suggestion that I can directly confront my essence in introspection, and that what I so encounter is a willing entity) is suspicious. Wasn't Kant correct, after all, that we cannot confront anything directly, that all knowledge is mediated by the forms of cognition?

Schopenhauer is not always clear on this point. Sometimes he says that the thing-in-itself, Will, is directly confronted, in a wholly noncognitive manner, when the subject experiences herself as a desirer and actor. For example, from *WWR*:

[O]n the path of *objective knowledge*, thus starting from the *representation*, we shall never get beyond the representation, i.e., the phenomenon. We shall therefore remain at the outside of things; we shall never be able to penetrate into their inner nature, and investigate what they are in themselves....So far, I agree with Kant. But now, as the counterpoise to this truth, I have stressed that other truth that we are not merely the *knowing subject*, but that *we ourselves are the thing-in-itself.* Consequently, a way *from within* stands open to us to that real inner nature of things to which we cannot penetrate *from without*. It is, so to speak, a subterranean passage, a secret alliance, which, as if by treachery, places us all at once in the fortress that could not be taken by attack from without. Precisely as such, the *thing-in-itself* can come into consciousness only quite directly, namely by *it itself being conscious of itself*; to try to know it objectively is to desire something contradictory. Everything objective is representation, consequently appearance; in fact mere phenomenon of the brain.[31]

Schopenhauer immediately qualifies this view, however:

[E]ven the inward observation we have of our own will still does not by any means furnish an exhaustive and adequate knowledge of the thing-in-itself. . . . For even in self-consciousness, the I is not absolutely simple, but consists of a knower (intellect) and a known (will); the former is not known and the latter is not knowing, although the two flow together into the consciousness of an I. But on this very account, this I is not *intimate* with itself through and through, does not shine through so to speak, but is opaque, and therefore remains a riddle to itself. Hence, even in inner knowledge there still occurs a difference between the being-in-itself of its object and the observation or perception of this object in the knowing subject. But the inner knowledge is free from two forms belonging to outer knowledge, the form of *space* and the form of *causality* which brings about all sense-perception. On the other hand, there still remains the form of *time*, as well as that of being known and of knowing in general. Accordingly, in this inner knowledge the thing-in-itself has indeed to a great extent cast off its veils, but still does not appear quite naked. In consequence of the form of time which still adheres to it, everyone knows his will only in its successive individual *acts*, not as a whole, in and by itself. Hence no one knows his character *a priori*, but he becomes acquainted with it only by way of experience and always imperfectly. Yet the apprehension in which we know the stirrings and acts of our own will is far more immediate than is any other. . . . Accordingly, the act of will is indeed only the nearest and clearest *phenomenon* of the thing-in-itself; yet it follows from this that, if all the other phenomena could be known by us just as immediately and intimately, we should be obliged to regard them precisely as that which the will is in us. Therefore in this sense I teach that the inner nature of every thing is *will*, and I call the will the thing-in-itself.[32]

As Christopher Janaway has noted, Schopenhauer reveals himself in these passages to be "caught between two stances, one bold, one

31. *WWR*, vol. 2, p. 195.
32. *WWR*, vol. 2, pp. 196–197.

circumspect."[33] With Janaway, I must conclude that the circumspect stance most clearly reflects Schopenhauer's mature view. According to Schopenhauer, introspective access to the thing-in-itself is not quite direct, though it operates through the sheerest of veils. There is another passage in *WWR*, a mysterious footnote inserted into volume 1, where Schopenhauer confronts the fact that the self encountered in introspection is, after all, only phenomenon, not noumenon. I love the spooky feel of this footnote, so I feel moved to quote it:

> On the one hand, every individual is the subject of knowing, in other words, the supplementary condition of the possibility of the whole objective world, and, on the other, a particular phenomenon of the will, of that will which objectifies itself in each thing. But this double character of our inner being does not rest on a self-existent unity, otherwise it would be possible for us to be conscious of ourselves *in ourselves and independently of the objects of knowing and willing.* Now we simply cannot do this, but as soon as we enter into ourselves in order to attempt it, and wish for once to know ourselves fully by directing our knowledge inwards, we lose ourselves in a bottomless void; we find ourselves like a hollow glass globe, from the emptiness of which a voice speaks. But the cause of this voice is not to be found in the globe, and since we want to comprehend ourselves, we grasp with a shudder nothing but a wavering and unstable phantom.[34]

We have seen that while Schopenhauer does argue for his great metaphysical conclusion, the argument is unsatisfactory. It is fairly clear that Schopenhauer was driven to his conclusion by a compelling personal experience (a mystical or religious experience) and that he attempted to buttress the conclusion with argument only after the fact. Schopenhauer tells his readers that his entire philosophy is an attempt to communicate a single thought. I believe that the single thought was an (ultimately unjustifiable) intuition of the unity of the inner nature of all things.

Besides the introspection-based argument just discussed, Schopenhauer has another argument for his great conclusion that the in-itself of all phenomena is Will. This other argument is based on

---

33. Christopher Janaway, "Will and Nature," in Janaway, ed., *The Cambridge Companion to Schopenhauer* (Cambridge: Cambridge University Press, 1999), p. 161.

34. *WWR*, vol. 1, p. 278 n. It is odd that this footnote is inserted in the midst of a discussion of death, where it does not obviously belong.

outer experience as opposed to inner experience, and is especially clear in Schopenhauer's essay *On the Will in Nature*.[35] Schopenhauer thinks that if we observe the natural world, it is evident that will (desire or striving after various goals) is operating within that world. This is the best explanation of why things behave as they do. This is perhaps clearest in the case of living nature. All living things strive to bring about such ends as nutrition, growth, survival, and reproduction. The goals of such striving are unconscious in most of nature. Typically, the goal is some event in the future of the striving organism. The organism never sees or contemplates the end of its activity. Nevertheless, the organism does things for the sake of these unconscious, future goals.

Schopenhauer liked to give such examples as these:

> The one-year-old bird has no notion of the eggs for which it builds a nest; the young spider has no idea of the prey for which it spins a web; the ant-lion has no notion of the ant for which it digs a cavity for the first time. The larva of the stag-beetle gnaws the hole in the wood, where it will undergo its metamorphosis; twice as large if it is to become a male beetle as if it is to become a female, in order in the former case to have room for the horns, though as yet it has no idea of these.[36]

Schopenhauer believed that such examples of animal instinct proved that the unconscious will of the animal was something noumenal, outside the forms of time, space, and causality imposed by cognition. How else could the individual animal act, obviously motivated by objects and events that did not yet exist in space and had not yet happened in time?

Nowadays, we are not supposed to believe in any will or teleology in nature. Biological orthodoxy declares that the chemical structure of DNA together with natural selection account for the kinds of behavior so impressive to Schopenhauer. Had Schopenhauer known about DNA and natural selection, would he have abandoned his insistence that observation reveals a will in nature? I doubt it. I believe he would have said that biological science is incomplete, and he would have had a point. Natural selection does not explain why

---

35. E. F. J. Payne's translation of *On the Will in Nature* was published by Berg in 1992. It is difficult to obtain in the United States. I thank my former student Robert Watson (a fellow Schopenhauer fan) for sending me a copy from France.

36. *WWR*, vol. I, p. 114.

complex nucleic acid molecules formed in the first place, or why they first "decided" to reproduce themselves. The hypothesis that all of nature, living and nonliving, is the manifestation of a Will, striving to express itself in all possible forms, at least gives us some clue as to how and why the complex systems we call "living" came about.

Schopenhauer extended his will-based understanding of nature to nonliving things. Notice that even today, chemists find it difficult to avoid attributing a certain "personality" to every element. Hydrogen "wants" to combine with oxygen to form water; the "noble gases" decline to mingle with very many other substances; and so on. For Schopenhauer, this is no metaphor. Each element *is* the will to combine with other substances in just these ways; its atomic structure is such a will made phenomenal. Indeed, every physical object is just the-will-to-do-X, as that will exists phenomenally. Schopenhauer's most vivid examples concern human body parts. Hands are the will to grasp; genitals are the will to copulate; the digestive tract is the will to eat. In general, Schopenhauer argues that the structure of things irresistibly suggests the metaphysical hypothesis of a will in nature, striving endlessly to express itself in endless variations of form and function.

Much has been said, by various commentators, regarding Schopenhauer's pessimism. If Schopenhauer is generally famous for anything these days, it is for having a grim view of life—for being a depressive, misanthropic old curmudgeon who believed "the game is not worth the candle."[37] It is true that Schopenhauer was self-consciously pessimistic. He thought optimism was silly, revealing a want of attention to the facts obviously revealed in experience. According to Schopenhauer, the nature of the Will reveals itself in the empirical world, and what we see when we investigate the empirical world is an endless striving, ever at odds with itself, never permanently satisfied. The essential nature of life is suffering. Here is a typical passage in which Schopenhauer reveals this point of view:

> Awakened to life out of the night of unconsciousness, the will finds itself as an individual in an endless and boundless world, among innumerable individuals, all striving, suffering, and erring; and, as if through a troubled dream, it hurries back to the old unconsciousness. Yet till then its desires are unlimited, its claims inexhaustible, and

---

37. Schopenhauer says "The game is not worth the candle" (in French) in *WWR*, vol. 2, p. 358.

every satisfied desire gives birth to a new one. No possible satisfaction in the world could suffice to still its craving, set a final goal to its demands, and fill the bottomless pit of its heart. In this connexion, let us now consider what as a rule comes to man in satisfactions of any kind; it is often nothing more than the bare maintenance of this very existence, exhorted daily with unremitting effort and constant care in conflict and misery and want, with death in prospect. Everything in life proclaims that earthly happiness is destined to be frustrated, or recognized as an illusion. The grounds for this lie deep in the very nature of things.... Life presents itself as a continual deception, in small matters as well as in great. If it has promised, it does not keep its word, unless to show how little desirable the desired object was; hence we are deluded now by hope, now by what was hoped for. If it has given, it did so in order to take. The enchantment of distance shows us paradises that vanish like optical illusions, when we have allowed ourselves to be fooled by them. Accordingly, happiness lies always in the future, or else in the past, and the present may be compared to a small dark cloud driven by the wind over a sunny plain; in front of and behind the cloud everything is bright, only it itself always casts a shadow.[38]

Because the blind, striving Will can never be satisfied, the only salvation possible for an individual lies in quieting his will, in ceasing to desire anything at all. This, however, is not something an individual can do voluntarily; in those to whom it happens, it just happens, because the Will has, in such individuals, reached its highest degree of objectification, and has (so to speak) burned itself out. It is notable that Schopenhauer himself never approached such a Nirvana-like state.[39]

Freedom, Determinism, and the Will

Schopenhauer's views on free will and determinism constitute an important part of his philosophical system. These views, while expressed inter alia in *WWR*, are most clearly and concisely set forth in Schopenhauer's *Prize Essay on the Freedom of the Will*.[40] I therefore devote this section to an overview of the latter work.

38. *WWR*, vol. 2, p. 573.

39. See the biography of Schopenhauer by Rudiger Safranski, *Schopenhauer and the Wild Years of Philosophy*, trans. Ewald Osers (Cambridge: Harvard University Press, 1989).

40. See note 9.

In April 1837, the announcement of an essay competition appeared in a German literary journal. The Royal Norwegian Society of Sciences was offering a prize for the best essay on the following topic: Can freedom of the will be proven from self-consciousness? Schopenhauer was then about fifty years old, and his two major works (*On the Fourfold Root of the Principle of Sufficient Reason* and *WWR*) had long been available to the philosophical public. These works, however, had failed to bring Schopenhauer any great acclaim. He took it upon himself to answer the essay question, using material that was already included in his previous works. He won the prize, and the prize brought some public attention to his ideas (to his great satisfaction).

Schopenhauer first distinguishes moral freedom, the sense of freedom most deeply relevant to the free will debate, from mere physical freedom. Physical freedom would be the absence of material obstacles in the way of acting in accordance with one's own will. Moral freedom, however, is popularly supposed to be something deeper. Schopenhauer notes that we may clarify the concept of moral freedom by taking it to be essentially opposed to necessity. We must now ask what "necessary" means, and here we find ourselves back in Schopenhauer's doctoral dissertation, *On the Fourfold Root of the Principle of Sufficient Reason.* According to Schopenhauer, "necessary" simply means following from a given sufficient ground. As I briefly sketched in a previous section, Schopenhauer believes that there are three basic kinds of sufficient grounds: physical/causal, conceptual/logical, and geometrical/mathematical. (Recall that the fourth type of explanation, explanation of action based on motive, is a variant of the first; it is physical causality "seen from within.") Something is explained when it follows from one of the three types of sufficient grounds. Being thus explainable is the mark of the phenomenon, the object-for-the-understanding. Accordingly, when we say that the will is free in the sense of moral freedom, we mean that acts of will follow from no sufficient ground whatever, and thus are unexplainable. Here is Schopenhauer:

> Now this concept, applied to the will of a human being, would state that in its manifestations (acts of will) an individual will would not be determined by causes or sufficient reasons in general.... [A] free will would be one that was determined by nothing at all. The particular manifestations of such a will (acts of will) would therefore proceed absolutely and quite originally from itself, without being brought about necessarily by antecedent conditions, and thus without

being determined by anything according to a rule. In the case of such a concept, clear thinking is at an end because the principle of sufficient reason in all its meanings is the essential form of our whole faculty of cognition, yet here it is supposed to be given up.[41]

Schopenhauer names this inexplicable ability to generate an action out of nothing *liberum arbitrium indifferentiae*, and says it is

the only clearly determined, firm, and settled concept of that which is called freedom of the will.... From the assumption of such a *liberum arbitrium indifferentiae*, the immediate consequence that characterizes this concept itself and is therefore to be stated as its mark is that for a human individual endowed with it, under given external circumstances that are determined quite individually and thoroughly, two diametrically opposed actions are equally possible.[42]

Recall that the question proposed by the Royal Society, to be answered by contest entrants, was: "Can freedom of the will be proven from self-consciousness?" Now that he has carefully defined (moral) freedom of the will, Schopenhauer defines self-consciousness.

Self-consciousness is whatever remains in consciousness after we have subtracted consciousness of outer things. The faculty concerned with consciousness of outer things, cognition, includes (in human beings) both (1) understanding and (2) reason. This dual faculty of cognition occupies by far the majority of human consciousness. The only thing left in consciousness when we subtract cognition is the awareness of our own desires, affects, emotions—all aspects of what Schopenhauer calls the *will*. These are, as Schopenhauer points out, always intimately tied up with outer things we desire either to possess or to avoid. It is a delicate operation to separate the will itself from its motives (as Schopenhauer calls the outer things that excite our feelings).

Self-consciousness, as opposed to the consciousness of other (outer) things, is quite limited, according to Schopenhauer. Remember, all motives and all conceptual thought belong to the faculty of cognition, concerned with outer things. If we try to put into words the content of self-consciousness (an attempt in itself misleading, since words belong to cognition), we get the phrase, "I can *do* what I *will*." As soon as I *will* in accordance with a particular motive, my body

41. Schopenhauer, *Prize Essay*, pp. 7–8.
42. Schopenhauer, *Prize Essay*, p. 8.

obeys. But this tells us nothing about moral freedom in the sense so carefully defined by Schopenhauer. "I can *do* what I *will*" expresses merely physical freedom, philosophically unproblematic. As to moral freedom—whether, in a given set of circumstances, the same person with the same character can *will* opposing acts—self-consciousness tells us nothing. As Schopenhauer puts it, "[S]elf-consciousness cannot even understand the question, much less answer it."[43]

Schopenhauer thus answers the Royal Society's question, "Can freedom of the will be proven from self-consciousness?" with a resounding "No!"

Schopenhauer believes that nothing in the phenomenal world occurs without a sufficient ground. All physical occurrences, including human actions, are necessary given their causes and antecedent conditions. In the case of a human action, the cause is confrontation with a motive, and the antecedent condition is the person's character.[44]

It is important to note that for Schopenhauer, the act of will and the bodily motion that carries it out are the noumenal and phenomenal aspects of one and the same event. We tend to think that first the act of will occurs, and then a corresponding body movement either does or does not carry it out. This is not how Schopenhauer sees it. According to Schopenhauer, what we *will*, we *do*, and it is the action that proclaims the genuine will (character) of the actor. Deliberation is just a process during which we wait to see which motive, ultimately, moves us to action. Moral freedom is an illusion.

We might well ask why the illusion is so powerful. Why do we have such a strong feeling that we had a "real choice," that we always could have done something other than what we did?

Schopenhauer's first answer is that we confuse wishing and willing. A given person, with a given character, in a given motivational situation, can *will* only one thing. She can, however, *wish* any number of different things: "[A]s long as the act of will is in the process of coming about, it is called *wish*.... Opposite wishes with their

---

43. Schopenhauer, *Prize Essay*, p. 14.

44. According to Schopenhauer, each person's individual character is a unique grade of objectification of Will, and therefore ontologically distinct. Each person is a Platonic Form unto itself. Nonhuman animals possess this uniqueness of individual character to a much lesser degree. In nonhuman animals, the character of the *species* is usually the force that interacts with motive to produce action.

motives pass up and down before [consciousness] alternately and repeatedly; about each of them it states that it will become the deed *if* it becomes the act of will."[45] The person involved in moral deliberation easily misses the hypothetical nature of her presumed freedom ("I *could* tell the truth and take the consequences, rather than lie about what happened to protect myself, *if* that were my strongest motive") and imagines that what she only wishes she could do, she really could do.

Schopenhauer's second explanation for the power of the illusion of moral freedom is more complex. It involves a comparison of human beings with less complex living things (nonhuman animals and plants).[46] We don't suppose that these "lower" creatures possess "free will" in the problematic philosophical sense. Why do we suppose that human creatures do? A plant obeys its natural stimulus and grows toward the light. We don't suppose that it is free to do otherwise. Quite rationally, we conclude that it couldn't have done otherwise unless something about it, or about its environment, had been different. Our pet cat tragically attacks and kills our pet bird. We don't morally blame the cat, supposing that it had a free choice. It is a cat, and a cat's nature is to hunt birds. We may regret the outcome, but we realize that the cat simply did what it is "programmed" to do, given the presence of the stimulus (the uncaged bird). We blame ourselves for not caging the bird, rather than blaming the cat. Why do we believe that we are different from the plant and the cat in possessing some mysterious freedom from causality, allegedly necessary for moral responsibility?

Schopenhauer's explanation is this: the necessitating causes of the behavior of plants and of nonhuman animals are easier to see, because of the simpler nature of these organisms. In the case of a stimulus–response system such as a plant, we clearly observe that the stimuli for its movements are changes in objects and forces in the external world—sunlight, water, and so on. In the case of a large-brained organism with representational powers such as a cat, we realize that the direct causes of its behavior are its representations or states of mind, but since its representations are always closely allied with its present environment, we clearly see that it reacts in predictable ways to predictable stimuli.

---

45. Schopenhauer, *Prize Essay*, p. 15. Emphasis on 'if' added.
46. Schopenhauer, *Prize Essay*, pp. 26–37.

Human beings, unlike all other known animals, possess *reason* in addition to *understanding*. This addition to our faculty of cognition enables the causal chains leading to our actions to become much more convoluted. Our representations are *not* always closely keyed to our present environment, because of our ability to employ abstract concepts. Thus, our actions may look mysterious to an outside observer. The outside observer cannot see the remembered past experiences, the anticipated future experiences, the wishes concerning what might be, the regrets regarding what has been, the desires to conform to abstract principles, and so forth, all of which enter into a human being's decisions. Accordingly, it may look as if the human being's actions are inexplicable and uncaused, but this is only an illusion stemming from the complexity of mental causes in human beings.[47]

Schopenhauer is quite clear on the point that the attribution of moral responsibility for action, far from presupposing causelessness, actually presupposes the causation of action by character and motive.[48] If a person's actions proceeded from absolutely nothing, rather than from his character, what would we condemn as vicious or praise as virtuous? Schopenhauer approvingly cites other philosophers who have come to this "soft determinist" or "compatibilist" conclusion.

Yet, if Schopenhauer were a typical compatibilist, we would expect him to say that when we impose punishments and bestow rewards, we are attempting to influence character for the better, by providing causes of character change. This Schopenhauer does *not* say. On the contrary, he says: "[T]he sphere and domain of all correction and improvement lie in *cognition* alone. The character is unalterable; the motives operate with necessity, but they have to pass through *cognition*, the medium of the motives."[49]

This requires some explanation. According to Schopenhauer, a person's character (his personality—how that person will tend to react to his environment) is inborn. Schopenhauer quotes Goethe: "From yourself you cannot flee." If we hope to change someone's behavior, we can do so *not* by altering his character (the latter would

---

47. Schopenhauer notes that a person's own determining motives may be hidden even from himself—one of many points on which Schopenhauer either influenced Freud or simply anticipated Freud.

48. Schopenhauer, *Prize Essay*, pp. 48–49.

49. Schopenhauer, *Prize Essay*, p. 45.

amount to the impossible action of making him into someone else), but only by teaching him the likely results of particular types of action and appealing to elements of his own "hard-wired" motivational structure.

There is another sophisticated wrinkle in Schopenhauer's position on freedom of the will, one that accounts for his choice of the motto "Freedom is a mystery" at the beginning of his prize essay. This wrinkle arises from Schopenhauer's transcendental idealism and from the enormous influence on him of many aspects of Kant's philosophy. Schopenhauer, despite rejecting "moral freedom" defined as the impossible *liberum arbitrium indifferentiae*, accepts that there really *is* such a thing as "*true* moral freedom," which he says is "of a higher kind."[50] He explains that our knowledge of the existence of such a "true" or "higher" moral freedom comes from

> the perfectly clear and certain feeling of *responsibility* for our actions—a feeling that rests on the unshakeable certainty that we ourselves are *the doers of our deeds*. On the strength of that consciousness, it never occurs to anyone, not even to someone who is fully convinced of the necessity with which our actions occur, to make use of this necessity as an excuse for a transgression, and to throw blame upon the motives because their appearance rendered the deed inevitable.... For he sees... [that] in existing circumstances and hence under the influence of the motives that have determined him, an entirely different action was quite possible and could have happened, *if only he had been another person*. Because he is this person and not another, because he has such-and-such a character, naturally no other action was possible for *him*.... Therefore the *responsibility* of which he is conscious... at bottom... concerns his *character*; it is for [his character] that he feels himself responsible....
>
> Where the guilt lies, there too lies the *responsibility*, and as the latter is the sole datum that justifies the inference to moral freedom, so too must freedom lie in that very place, hence in the *character* of the human being.[51]

But how can freedom lie in character? Hasn't Schopenhauer already told us that character is inborn and unalterable?

The answer to this puzzle lies in Schopenhauer's appeal to a Kantian distinction between empirical character and intelligible character. Our empirical character is how our will manifests itself

---

50. Schopenhauer, *Prize Essay*, p. 83.
51. Schopenhauer, *Prize Essay*, pp. 84–85.

in the phenomenal world. But we mustn't forget that, according to Schopenhauer, we are aware of our own will in a direct (or, rather, nearly direct) way, via self-consciousness, that involves the forms of cognition only minimally. When we experience ourselves as subjects of will, we experience the thing-in-itself as immediately as possible. This thing-in-itself is the force that manifests itself as our character. It is our essence, upon which all our actions (in some sense) depend. Even though our own empirical character is something we come to know only after the fact, by years of self-observation, our intelligible character, our essence, is that with which we are most intimately acquainted, from the very beginning of our lives. It cannot possibly be subject to causation because it is noumenal, not phenomenal.

Because I know myself as the willer of my own deeds, I feel ownership or responsibility for those deeds. Those deeds proceed from *me*, from who I am in my inmost being. By observing my own deeds over a lifetime, I find out who I am. But I also know that I, as a will (a unique manifestation of the thing-in-itself), am free. I am one of the essential natural forces that are presupposed by all causal relations and causal explanations. Ultimately, it can no more be explained why I act than it can be explained why a magnetic field changing in the presence of a conductor generates an electric current. The basic forces of nature are where causal explanation stops. These forces themselves, because presupposed by causal explanation, are not themselves subject to causation: they are free. "Freedom is transcendental," concludes Schopenhauer.[52] This is the "mystery."

He puts the point differently, certainly more colorfully, in *WWR*. This is a lovely passage from Schopenhauer, one of my favorites: "Spinoza says that if a stone projected through the air had consciousness, it would imagine it was flying of its own will. I merely add that the stone would be right."[53] What Schopenhauer means is that the thing-in-itself (whatever it is that exists outside the forms imposed by our own cognition) manifests itself in nonliving systems as physical forces, and in living systems as will. This thing-in-itself is transcendentally free at least in the sense of being prior to causality and presupposed by all causal explanations. As Schopenhauer repeatedly puts it, freedom of the will is very real and of paramount

---

52. Schopenhauer, *Prize Essay*, p. 88.
53. *WWR*, vol. 1, p. 126.

metaphysical importance—but it belongs not to the *operations* of the will; rather, it belongs to the *essence* of the will.[54]

The Basis of Ethics: Reason versus Compassion

Besides his prize essay on freedom of the will, Schopenhauer wrote another essay that he hoped would similarly be "crowned" by winning a prize. This time, his hopes were not fulfilled. Schopenhauer's short work *On the Basis of Morality*[55] was written in 1839 as his entry in a contest sponsored by the Royal Danish Society of Scientific Studies. The contest invited answers to the following question: "Are the source and foundation of morals to be looked for in an idea of morality lying immediately in consciousness (or conscience) and in the analysis of the other fundamental moral concepts springing from that idea, or are they to be looked for in a different ground of knowledge?"

Schopenhauer's essay was the sole entry received by the society. The board of judges declined to award Schopenhauer the prize, claiming that he had failed to address the proper question (the relationship between metaphysics and ethics) and that he had abused and insulted other distinguished philosophers. The latter charge was not altogether false. All of Schopenhauer's writings, including the essay on ethics, contain vituperative abuse of Hegel, whom Schopenhauer envied and despised. Schopenhauer was also unable to disguise his contempt for Kant's ethical theory, which he believed to be utterly ungrounded.

Kant famously claims, in his *Groundwork of the Metaphysics of Morals*, that pure reason contains or reveals a moral law: the "categorical imperative" according to which rational beings may never use rational beings as means to ends. Lying, stealing, and killing are wrong because one thereby uses other people as means to one's ends; suicide is wrong because one thereby uses oneself as a means to an end. According to Kant, the very contemplation of a violation

---

54. In my opinion, no one has ever written anything on the problem of free will and determinism clearer or more persuasive than Schopenhauer's *Prize Essay*. The only development since Schopenhauer's time that might possibly cast doubt on his conclusions is the advent of nondeterministic quantum mechanics.

55. See Schopenhauer, *On the Basis of Morality*, trans. E. F. J. Payne, introduction by David E. Cartwright (Indianapolis: Hackett, 1995).

of this rule involves the agent in a contradiction within his own will. Disobeying the categorical imperative is therefore irrational. Kant's attempts to demonstrate the contradiction are notoriously unsuccessful, and Schopenhauer argues that not only is there no contradiction involved in violating the alleged moral law, but there is no a priori moral law in terms of a contentful rule. If anything about ethics is a priori, it is the mere empty form of a rule. Perhaps it is necessary that rational beings should be capable of conscious rule following, but exactly what rules they should follow is nowhere given. Furthermore, all rules are hypothetical imperatives, taking the form "do this *if* you want to achieve such-and-such a result." The notion of a categorical imperative—a rule that one must follow merely in virtue of being a creature capable of following rules—is a fiction, conjured by Kant out of thin air in order to bolster Kant's rationally ungrounded Christian convictions.

Schopenhauer offers, in contrast to Kant's attempt to ground ethics in a priori reason, the theory that ethics is grounded in compassion. The basis of moral action, according to Schopenhauer, is the quasi-mystical intuition of the oneness of all things. Because all creatures are manifestations of the same Will, the suffering Other is ultimately identical with one's Self. The ancient Indian doctrine of *tat tvam asi* ("that art thou") is, for Schopenhauer, the metaphysical truth lurking behind our deepest moral intuitions.

CHAPTER TWO

Three Major Themes of Schopenhauer's Philosophy

Transcendental Idealism, Panpsychism, and Determinism

I have attempted to give an overview of Schopenhauer's thought in chapter 1. I now wish to focus on some major themes, elaborate on them, and evaluate their overall plausibility. My position is that Schopenhauer's philosophy becomes much more attractive when we jettison the Kantian framework, drawing out and retaining the elements in Schopenhauer hostile to idealism. However, I first sketch Kant's transcendental idealism and consider how Schopenhauer's version of idealism differs from it.

Kant's Epistemology

Kant wanted something more out of science than just theories that have not yet proven false. Kant wanted science to be able to formulate absolute, nonrevisable truths, and he believed that the science of his day had done just this, in the discovery of Newtonian laws of physics. Kant asked himself how this was possible, and he figured out that an empiricist theory of knowledge, such as Hume's, was not up to the job.

According to Kant, the pure empiricism of Hume leads to an unsatisfactory sort of skepticism. If the only materials for knowledge are sense-data, or "ideas" coming in through the senses, stuck together by purely psychological principles of association, then we can't know much of anything at all. We cannot tell the difference between a real causal connection and an accidental regularity that has merely held so far in our experience. Hence, we can never know what the genuine laws of nature are. We cannot know that we ourselves exist, apart from bundles of sense perceptions. We cannot know that there is any nonmental substance (matter).

What about the rationalism of Plato, Descartes, Leibniz, and Spinoza? These systems all seemed to Kant to involve unjustifiable flights of metaphysical fancy. Each rationalist insists that mathematics and geometry describe mind-independent reality, but none manages to explain how we can be sure of it. Likewise, each insists that a priori reason leads to certain conclusions about the nature of reality—but each rationalist's "certain" conclusions contradict the conclusions of the others! Is there one substance? Two? An infinity? Something has gone wrong somewhere, Kant thinks; this is "dogmatism" or "enthusiasm," not soberly justifiable knowledge.

Kant proposes to steer the ship of knowledge between the Scylla of skepticism and the Charybdis of dogmatism. The way to do this, he says, is by working a "Copernican Revolution" in our conception of knowledge itself. It is natural to regard inquiry as the attempt to make our ideas match reality. Kant's ingenious (and perverse) move is to say that it is really the other way around. When we genuinely achieve knowledge, says Kant, we are bringing reality into line with our own ideas. All scientific knowledge is anchored in the synthetic a priori—truths about the world that cannot help but be true because they are "hard-wired" into us, such as mathematical truths and the idea that every event must have a cause.

Kant turned out to be wrong, at least in the details. He declared some things to be synthetic a priori, hard-wired into us and therefore necessarily true that later turned out to be false. He imagined (understandably, at the time) that certain principles of Newtonian physics were absolutely true and could not be overturned, and that space was necessarily described by Euclidean geometry.

Despite these errors, does it remain possible that Kant's general point was correct—that there are innate constraints within our minds to which any science or reasoning we achieve must conform?

Perhaps. I have long struggled with this. Often, it seems to me that Kant must be right, at least to some extent. Surely our cognitive structure places some kind of limits on what we can know and how we can know it. But even if there are built-in constraints on knowledge, is there any a priori way to find out what those constraints are? Is there any sure way to tell what's coming from our minds and what's coming from the world? I doubt it. I continue to prefer a kind of pragmatic empiricism—let science go where it will, with nothing sacred and everything up for grabs, and find out what happens—to the risky pretensions of transcendental philosophy.

It is important to note that Kant rejected certain sorts of idealism, such as Berkeley's, as unsatisfactory. Kant believed his own "transcendental" idealism to be superior to other versions. In the section of *Critique of Pure Reason* titled "Refutation of Idealism," Kant takes Berkeley and Descartes as his opponents and argues that our experience of ourselves in time necessarily involves experience of objects outside us in space. This argument is worth looking at in detail, since in attempting to distinguish his own idealism from other versions, Kant unintentionally succeeds in undermining any kind of idealism, including his own.[1]

Kant calls Descartes a "problematical idealist" and says Descartes declares the existence of objects outside us to be doubtful and indemonstrable. Kant calls Berkeley a "dogmatic idealist," since Berkeley declares that the objects directly encountered in experience are mere ideas, thereby making space and matter into empirically unjustifiable hypotheses.

Taking himself to be arguing against Descartes, Kant says: "[It must be shown that] we have *experience*, and not merely imagination, of outer things; and this...cannot be achieved save by proof that even our inner experience, which for Descartes is indubitable, is possible only on the assumption of *outer* experience."[2]

In calling Descartes a "problematical idealist" and in thinking Descartes does not establish the existence of objects in space outside us, Kant misunderstands Descartes. Descartes never seriously doubts the existence of extended substance; his doubt is entirely methodological. Furthermore, Descartes has his own argument for the same conclusion Kant reaches in his "Refutation of Idealism," namely, that objects in space must exist outside us. In the context of his ontological argument in Meditation 3, Descartes concludes that there must exist enough mind-independent reality to account for

1. See Kant, *Critique of Pure Reason*, trans. Norman Kemp Smith (New York: St. Martin's, 1965), pp. 244–247.

2. Kant, *Critique of Pure Reason*, p. 244. It is important to note that, for Kant, space is ideal, so anything *in* space is ideal. Spatial objects, while ideal, are "outside" us in that they are at a spatial distance from our bodies.

the content of all our ideas. Descartes never doubts that this mind-independent reality includes extended substance.

Let me clarify what it is for a thing to be *real*. I approve of John Heil's way of putting it: you are a realist about x if you take x to be mind independent, and x is mind independent just in case its existence does not depend on its being thought about.[3] Heil points out that anti-realism about something always presupposes realism about something else. Consider Berkeley, for instance. Berkeley is an anti-realist about material bodies, but a realist about minds and their contents. But wait! How could *minds* be mind independent? They are mind independent in the sense that their existence does not depend on their being thought about. The same holds for *ideas*: an idea exists quite independently of its being thought about. (A particular idea, for Berkeley, is there whether or not you have an idea *of it*.) Realism, then, requires mind independence, but it does not require the existence of a nonmental reality. We might all be images in a dream flowing from the nostrils of Vishnu, but then that dream (and the dreamer, Vishnu) must be mind independent.

Let us return now to consideration of Descartes's *Meditations*. Descartes's appeal to God as the warrant for our most clear and distinct ideas is an elaborate subterfuge. It is notorious that the appeal to God is circular, since we must rely on clear and distinct ideas in order to argue for the existence of God, anyway. Descartes expected his more astute readers to know that he was too smart to make a blatantly circular argument.[4] Insofar as Descartes believes in God at all, his God *just is* clear and distinct conception, taken without limits (an "infinite, thinking substance"). When Descartes says "God is not a deceiver," he means that when we use clear and distinct conception (i.e., logical, mathematical, and geometrical reasoning), we cannot be wrong. He is laying down, as the foundational plank in his epistemology, the thesis that deductive reasoning is the most reliable of all human faculties. Indeed, it is a perfect faculty; if you use it at all, you are using it right. Unless we possessed such a faculty, Descartes thinks, knowledge would be impossible.

3. See John Heil, *From an Ontological Point of View* (Oxford: Oxford University Press, 2003), pp. 58–59. This view on realism and anti-realism also stems from the work of C. B. Martin.

4. See Descartes's Letter of Dedication in *Meditations*. Descartes says that few people will be able to understand what he is really saying.

If we take out all the confusing terminology, Descartes's most compelling version of the ontological argument may be paraphrased as follows: Here I am, thinking about reality in general. Thoughts are mental representations. Mental representations must originally derive their content from some mind independent reality. Thought (at least when it lacks the clarity and distinctness of math and geometry) may distort the nature of this mind-independent reality, but still, there must exist enough reality to account for the content of all my thoughts. The idea of God, being the idea of an unlimited thinking substance, has more content than any other idea, but again, there must exist enough mind-independent reality to account for the content of all my ideas, including the idea of God. So, God exists as a mind-independent reality.[5]

So far, Descartes has not established the existence of an extended substance and so has not established the existence of objects in space outside us. It is clear, however, that he never doubts that a great many of our ideas are about an extended substance. For example, he states that corporeal nature is the object of pure mathematics.[6]

While this is tangential to my main point, it is interesting to note that the ontological argument is not an argument for the existence of God, at least if one takes "God" in the normal, religious sense; it is an argument for the existence of mind-independent reality. The way to make the ontological argument work is to conceive of God as the sum total of mind-independent reality.[7] Spinoza, for example, endorses a version of the ontological argument: God's existence follows from God's conceivability. But Spinoza thinks of God as unlimited reality, both thinking and extended; and, for Spinoza, to say that God is perfect is just to say that God is real (see *Ethics*, pt. I, def. 6, where Spinoza explicitly states that by "God" he means

---

5. See Descartes, Meditation 3. Descartes's term for mental content is "objective reality." This is confusing to the uninitiated.

6. See the last line of Meditation 5: "But now it is possible for me to achieve full and certain knowledge about countless things, both about God and other intellectual matters, as well as about the entirety of that corporeal nature which is the object of pure mathematics." I quote here the translation by Donald A. Cress (Indianapolis: Hackett, 1993).

7. Bertrand Russell relates in his autobiography that one day he was walking across campus and realized, "Great God in boots! The ontological argument is sound!" I had a similar experience when I realized that the ontological argument isn't really about God at all; it's about mind-independent reality. See Russell, *The Autobiography of Bertrand Russell, 1872–1914* (Boston: Little-Brown, 1967), p. 84.

unlimited reality, and *Ethics*, pt. II, def. 6, where he states that by "perfect" he means "real").

The most common objection to the ontological argument is that one can never give an a priori, logical proof of the *existence* of something. Existence claims, it is said, require empirical evidence, not merely armchair argumentation. This is a good objection to any attempt to prove a priori the existence of this or that particular object. Indeed, from the fact that I can conceive of a unicorn, it does not follow that a unicorn must actually exist. However, from the fact that I can think at all, it does follow that something exists (mind-independent reality in general) in order that I might have something to think *about*.

The ontological argument, in other words, is really an argument against epistemic skepticism and is essentially the same argument made by modern proponents of "content externalism" in the philosophy of mind: ultimately, our thoughts cannot have content unless they refer to something outside us. One such externalist, Hilary Putnam, perhaps endorses a slightly softer line. He says that the content of a thought is whatever causes it. Putnam notes that the cause of a thought could be purely mental—my thought of a tree could be caused by a tree image. But Putnam's work goes on irresistibly to raise the question: How could there be a tree image unless there existed trees, or at least realities (e.g., mind-independent matter) to account for the basic components of trees?[8]

Think for a moment about Leibniz's version of the ontological argument. Leibniz argues that there must be a sufficient reason for the existence of the entire infinite series of contingent beings, whose individual sufficient reasons are other contingent beings. This ultimate sufficient reason cannot be another contingent being; it must be a necessary being. The necessary being has the "privilege" that if it is possible, it is necessary.[9] The latter statement is obscure. How

8. See Hilary Putnam, "Brains in a Vat," reprinted in Michael Huemer, ed., *Epistemology: Contemporary Readings* (London: Routledge, 2002), pp. 524–538. It perplexes me that Putnam, in other work, defends anti-realism and the concomitant view that metaphysics is about our concepts, not about the structure of the mind-independent world. These two parts of Putnam's philosophy seem inconsistent.

9. See Leibniz, *Monadology*, reprinted in Daniel Garber and Roger Ariew, eds., *Discourse on Metaphysics and Other Essays* (Indianapolis: Hackett, 1991), secs. 36–45. Notice that Leibniz's view makes clear the following point: to be mind independent, a substance need not be either extended or nonmental. Monads, for Leibniz, are

can the existence of a necessary being follow from its mere conceivability (possibility)? The only way I can figure out to make this intelligible is to take God (the necessary being) to be the sum total of mind-independent reality. Perhaps Leibniz means that if you can conceive of mind-independent reality at all, then the very existence of the thought proves that mind-independent reality exists. Again, thought obviously exists, and thought must be *about* something. Thought would have no content unless there were something to think *about*. (Of course, there are problems with this interpretation of Leibniz. Leibniz implies in various places that God is a monad who creates the other monads.[10] This conflicts with the notion that God is the sum total of mind-independent reality. Fortunately, it is beyond the scope of this discussion to make Leibniz entirely consistent.)

Descartes's position is that God is a thinking substance, and therefore not extended. No property of God is a mode of extension, and no extended mode is a perfection. So, his version of the ontological argument cannot be taken by itself to establish the existence of extended substance. We must supplement it with other things Descartes says. However (my main point), it is clear that Descartes was not a "problematical idealist" in Kant's sense. He never really doubts that extended substance, and therefore physical objects, are real and exist in space outside us.[11]

Taken as a response to Berkeley, however, Kant's argument may seem to be aimed at a more appropriate target. According to Berkeley, empiricism demands that we come to the following conclusion: reality consists only of ideas and the minds entertaining the ideas. However, does this make Berkeley a "dogmatic idealist," someone who thinks other people, tables, chairs, and so on, are not objects in space outside us? (Remember that, for Berkeley, both ideas and minds are real, that is, mind independent, in the sense relevant to our inquiry.)

---

elementary minds, and they are not extended; extension is a mere dream of the monads. Nevertheless, the existence of a monad does not depend on its being thought about by another monad, so monads are mind independent.

10. See, for example, *Monadology*, sec. 47, where Leibniz says, "Thus God alone is the primitive unity or the first simple substance; all created or derivative monads are products and are generated, so to speak, by continual fulgurations of the divinity."

11. I am grateful to Abraham "Brom" Anderson and to John Heil for clarifying my understanding of Descartes.

Here is Kant's argument:

> I am conscious of my own existence as determined in time. All determination of time presupposes something *permanent* in perception. But this permanent [thing] cannot be an intuition in me. For all grounds of determination of my existence which are to be met with in me are representations, and, as representations, themselves require a permanent [thing] distinct from them, in relation to which their change, and so my existence in the time wherein they change, may be determined. Thus, perception of this permanent [thing] is possible only through a *thing* outside me and not through the mere *representation* of a thing outside me; and consequently the determination of my existence in time is possible only through the existence of actual things which I perceive outside me.... In other words, the consciousness of my existence is at the same time an immediate consciousness of the existence of other things outside me.[12]

When Kant says, "I am conscious of my own existence as determined in time," what exactly does he mean? He seems to mean that I am aware of myself as a finite and temporary being, one who comes to exist, changes, and then eventually passes out of existence. This presupposes a relatively stable world outside my own mind, by reference to which I could see myself coming into this world, interacting with it, and eventually leaving it. Part of the point seems to be that I experience myself as an *actor*. *Action* is inevitably *interaction* with things and events in the external world. It is these things and events that serve as the goals and motivators of action. When Kant says, "All determination of time presupposes something permanent in perception," part of his meaning may be that the goals and motivators of my actions do not pop into and out of existence, as they would if they were just my subjective ideas. I can rely on objects and events in the external world to exhibit a certain stability; otherwise, action in pursuit of goals would be futile and would make no sense.

Perhaps the deeper point is that perception is constrained by the noumena (though not wholly constrained). When Kant says that "representations...require a permanent [thing] distinct from them, in relation to which their change, and so my existence in the time wherein they change, may be determined," he means that the character of my perception is a function of how I am and how the world

12. Kant, *Critique of Pure Reason*, p. 245.

is. The trouble is, I have no access to how the world is outside of my perceptions, so I cannot infer its properties from their appearances. Let us consider an example of ordinary, everyday action. Suppose I feel hungry and decide to eat a buttered baked potato I happen to know is in my refrigerator. I go the refrigerator, retrieve the potato, heat it up in the microwave oven, and proceed to eat it. All this is necessarily temporal—it involves one event succeeding another. It also necessarily involves interaction with more-or-less permanent things in my environment. If the potato were merely my subjective idea, it seems it would cease to exist while lying unperceived in the refrigerator. Likewise, if the potato were merely my subjective idea, it is hard to understand how it could nourish me after I consumed it.[13] Again, perhaps the deep point concerns not action, but perception. If the potato were wholly a construct, the perceiver would be responsible for the whole fabric of reality (and that seems crazy). The mind might color, structure, and so forth, my perceptions, but surely the world constrains their general features.

Briefly: my awareness of myself as a living being (an actor and perceiver) depends on the existence of permanent objects in the external world and my ability to interact with those objects.

It has often seemed to me that Kant, in his "refutation of idealism," has effectively undermined his own idealism, along with Berkeley's. I have never understood clearly what is supposed to be the big difference between Kantian "transcendental" idealism and Berkelean idealism, anyway. Kant tries to explain it by saying that, for him (as opposed to Berkeley), material objects and the space in which they exist are "*empirically* real but *transcendentally* ideal." I can't, for the life of me, understand what that is supposed to mean. If objects are real enough to bump into me, to hurt me, to nourish me when I eat them, and so on, in what sense are they ideal? As for the space in which objects exist, how can I know for sure that space is a form of experience supplied by the mind, and not something completely mind independent?

---

13. Russell makes a similar point against idealism: suppose my cat gets hungry. If my cat is a collection of ideas, it becomes completely inexplicable why the cat gets hungry. Ideas are "as incapable of getting hungry as a triangle is of playing football." My related point is that if the cat's food were merely ideas, it becomes utterly inexplicable how those ideas could nourish the cat. See Russell, *The Problems of Philosophy* (Buffalo: Prometheus Books, 1988). The passage about the cat occurs on p. 23, in the chapter titled "The Existence of Matter."

Perhaps I can get at the difference (or at least *a* difference) between Berkelean and Kantian idealism by imagining Berkeley and Kant arguing with each other:

> BERKELEY: Yes, there is mind-independent reality; it consists of minds and their contents. Minds in no way depend on their being perceived. If you think I'm a 'dogmatic idealist' in the sense that I deny the existence of mind-independent reality, you're just *wrong*.
>
> KANT: If *all* that exists are minds and their contents, how do we account for the evident fact that our perceptions are constrained? It's implausible to think they are constrained only by *us*.

We are left with two possibilities: (a) there exists some nonmental reality; (b) there exists a God, and objects are ideas in the mind of God. Kant opts for the former; Berkeley opts for the latter. I go with Kant. But then, again, it seems to me that Kant has undermined his own idealism.

Schopenhauer's Version of Idealism and His Evaluation of Kant

I find it useful at this point, for purposes of clarity and organization, to summarize Schopenhauer's views and his disagreements with Kant. This necessitates some repetition of material already covered in chapter 1.

Schopenhauer calls attention to the fact that there is a deep agreement among Kant, Plato, and the wisdom of ancient India. The world accessible to the senses, the source of empirical data, is merely the "veil of Maya," an illusion, a mask hiding a deeper reality beyond. What lies beyond is a riddle.

So far, so good. What lies beyond our ideas is indeed a riddle. However, Schopenhauer purports to solve the riddle, at least in part, by adopting idealism. He says, in effect, that our ideas *are* the world. *The world is my representation*, after all, is the first line of *The World as Will and Representation*. He declares that there is no world at all (no structure characterized by individuation, time, space, and causality) until the first eye opens. Thus, he places himself in the Kantian camp. Schopenhauer, in fact, declares himself an even more virulent idealist than Kant. He criticizes Kant for being a wishy-washy idealist and says he wants to return to a purer idealism more like Berkeley's.[14]

Schopenhauer acknowledges his debt to Kant. He specifies the following as Kant's great merits: (1) Kant drew the distinction between phenomenon and thing-in-itself. Like Berkeley, Kant made the move to idealism by correcting Locke's error of attributing primary qualities to things-in-themselves.[15] (2) Kant saw that human conduct has a moral significance that somehow touches on the thing-in-itself.[16] (3) Kant overthrew Scholasticism and the dependence of philosophy on religious dogma by showing that nothing about God, immortality, and so forth, would ever be proven.[17] (4) Kant drew the distinction between empirical character, which is causally determined, like every other phenomenon, and intelligible character, which, being noumenal, is outside causality, therefore free.[18] Furthermore, Kant eliminates the mysticism of Plato and declares that insofar as we may be certain of anything (mathematics; geometry; logic; that space, time, and material substance exist; that every event has a cause) we achieve this certainty only because we are describing our own a priori structures of thought.[19]

Despite his merits, Kant made some "great errors,"[20] according to Schopenhauer.

First error: According to Kant, the source of metaphysical knowledge cannot be empirical; neither inner nor outer intuition can tell us anything about the thing-in-itself (or about any other metaphysical matter, e.g., God, immortality, and freedom). In general, Kant despairs of metaphysical knowledge, since it would transcend all experience. For Kant, traditional metaphysics is the realm of faith, not knowledge. The only useful philosophical activity, for Kant, is "critique," determining the a priori contributions of our minds to knowledge.

---

14. See Schopenhauer, *The World as Will and Representation* (hereafter *WWR*), vol. 1, appendix, "Criticism of the Kantian Philosophy," pp. 434–435.

15. *WWR*, vol. 1, appendix, p. 418.

16. *WWR*, vol. 1, appendix, p. 422.

17. *WWR*, vol. 1, appendix, pp. 422–423.

18. *WWR*, vol. 1, appendix, p. 505. Schopenhauer declares Kant's discussion of the contrast between the empirical and intelligible characters to be "among the most admirable things ever said by man."

19. *WWR*, vol. 1, appendix, pp. 419–421.

20. *WWR*, vol. 1, appendix, p. 425.

Schopenhauer disagrees. He believes metaphysical knowledge is possible and that the source of metaphysical knowledge is the same as the source of scientific knowledge—observation and experience, including introspection. He believes that the solution to "the riddle of the world," which would be metaphysical knowledge, is to be found at the meeting point between inner and outer experience (between sensation and introspection). We can find out about the nature of the thing-in-itself by looking at that which is not the thing-in-itself.[21]

Second error: Kant posits twelve categories, which are (roughly) logical forms of judgment. Kant holds that we need all these categories in order to have experience of a world. This implies that non-human animals (which do not possess language and therefore do not make judgments with logical forms) do not experience themselves as living in a world.

The implication is false, according to Schopenhauer. Nonhuman animals clearly understand cause–effect relations, and that is all that is necessary in order to have meaningful experience. Schopenhauer claims that the only category we need is cause and effect. Application of this category is the business of "the understanding," the cognitive faculty shared by humans with nonhuman animals. In general, Schopenhauer says, Kant fails to distinguish between (a) understanding, or perceptual knowledge, and (b) reason, or conceptual knowledge. Logic and language are required only for the latter.[22]

Third error: Kant is ambivalent about his own idealism, according to Schopenhauer. In the first edition of the *Critique of Pure Reason*, Kant openly endorsed the notion that there can be no object without a subject, and his position was not too far from Berkeley's. But in the second edition of *Critique*, Kant developed a fear of Berkelean idealism and said all sorts of confusing and apparently contradictory things (e.g., both that the "object of experience" is independent of the understanding, and that the understanding is necessary in order to create this object).[23]

Schopenhauer argues that Kant should have been forthright about his idealism and openly said that the empirical world is entirely representation. Instead, Kant seems to have "an old, deep-rooted

21. *WWR*, vol. 1, appendix, pp. 426–428.
22. *WWR*, vol. 1, appendix, p. 439.
23. *WWR*, vol. 1, appendix, pp. 434–437.

prejudice"[24] to the effect that there really *is* an absolute object, an object without a subject.

Fourth error: Kant constantly uses the phrase "the object of experience." This object is supposed to be the proper subject of the categories. According to Kant, it is not the representation of perception, nor is it the abstract concept, so what is it? It is, according to Schopenhauer's reading of Kant, "different from both, yet both at the same time."[25]

According to Schopenhauer, Kant never made clear what he had in mind as the object of experience. Schopenhauer thinks Kant did not really have anything clearly in mind.

Fifth error: Kant rejected empiricism too completely. The empiricists were correct that perception furnishes all the material for thought. Without perception, there is no content to thought, either scientific or philosophical. Pure reason contains only empty forms—no objects, no judgments.[26]

Schopenhauer moves away from Kant, in an empiricist direction, by insisting that thought-forms can have no content unless that content comes from experience. For example, as I discuss in more detail in chapter 3, Schopenhauer denies that pure reason could be the source of the ethical principle Kant calls "the categorical imperative."

Sixth error: Kant believed action motivated by compassion had no moral value.[27]

This is precisely wrong, according to Schopenhauer. Schopenhauer thinks the basis of all moral action is compassion (again, I discuss this in more detail in chapter 3).

Some of Schopenhauer's criticisms of Kant strike me as correct. Indeed, Kant posited an excessive number of categories and did not appreciate the cognitive abilities of nonlinguistic animals. Kant did reject empiricism too completely. The source of metaphysical knowledge is indeed the same as the source of scientific knowledge. However, when Schopenhauer approves of idealism and takes Kant to task for not being idealist enough, I think Schopenhauer is going in the wrong direction.

24. *WWR*, vol. 1, appendix, p. 442.
25. *WWR*, vol. 1, appendix, p. 437.
26. *WWR*, vol. 1, appendix, pp. 450–451.
27. *WWR*, vol. 1, appendix, p. 526.

Why I Am Not an Idealist

I have considered idealism over the years, and for a time was seduced by it. Ultimately, however, I have rejected it. Can I justify my anti-idealist stance, or is anti-idealism versus idealism[28] one of those ground-level philosophical dichotomies where neither side can be better justified than the other? All I can do is give the arguments that ultimately swayed me, admitting that the ability of these arguments to sway me probably indicates more about my character than it does about the truth of the matter.

The passage where Schopenhauer introduces his "antinomy" makes my head spin, and I must come out on the side of the scientific realist rather than the transcendental idealist. The idea that space, time, and causality come into being only when living, sensing beings appear seems immediately paradoxical: How could there have been no time before such beings came along? Imagine a volcano erupting on the lifeless earth, long ago, prior to the existence of organisms. Surely, the eruption occurs at a time, and is a definite event. It need not await the appearance of organisms before becoming time-bound and individuated. The nature of time and individuation are indeed metaphysical puzzles, but just how are they solved by adopting transcendental idealism? Transcendental idealism suggests, in a way offensive to the scientific mind, that the whole vast, mysterious universe somehow depends on us and our puny minds. That's just too much hubris for me.

Could Berkeley be correct that I am covertly smuggling a subject into the picture when I imagine a lifeless world? Well, I am imagining how such a world would look, feel, and so on, so maybe I am covertly smuggling in a perceiver. Berkeley's argument is not conclusively refuted by the glib observation: just because the picture is in a subject (me) it doesn't follow that there is a subject in the picture.

28. It is important to keep one's terminology straight and not to conflate anti-realism and idealism. One can be an idealist and still be a realist in the sense of endorsing mind-independent reality; we have seen that Berkeley is an example. We have also seen that being an anti-realist about x presupposes being a realist about something else. Despite these complications, it is common for philosophers to speak in terms of a dichotomy between realists, who are said to believe in a mind-independent reality, and idealists or anti-realists, who are said to believe that everything depends on mind. This alleged dichotomy is a confusion and gives rise to confused (and confusing) conversations.

Idealists insist that no object can exist without a subject. Well, maybe. But how do we know? It seems a perfectly reasonable metaphysical hypothesis that objects might exist without subjects. I have decided to bet on the latter hypothesis (maybe because of my faith in science).

I am inclined to endorse a "truth-maker principle": if a claim is true, there must exist something that makes it true.[29] I also endorse the ontological argument, properly understood as the point that thought would have no content unless there existed mind-independent reality to be the content of thought. However, as we have seen, an idealist like Berkeley can hold to a truth-maker principle and the existence of mind-independent reality. Berkelean idealism and scientific realism appear to be alternative hypotheses, each accounting for exactly the same evidence, so no definitive rational grounds exist for choosing between them.

It is often said that empiricism collapses into idealism because of the crucial error of thinking that in experience we confront only ideas, not real objects. People say this is what happened to Berkeley, and (to his dismay) Hume. To suppose that we are trapped in a world of our own ideas, not in epistemic contact with real things, is to take the fatal step toward epistemic hell. This is the line taken by direct realists in epistemology, such as Thomas Reid, G. E. Moore, and J. L. Austin.[30] If, with these thinkers, we accept at the outset the commonsense belief that experience presents us with real objects, we can proceed without incoherence to inquire into the inner nature of those objects. In other words, we can do science and metaphysics in the old-fashioned way, as the investigation of the structure of mind-independent reality. On the other hand, if we decide that experience presents us only with ideas, what are we inquiring into when we do science and metaphysics? The content of our own ideas? But our ideas can have no content unless they obtain that content from something real beyond them.

Kant's suggestion that legitimate metaphysical inquiry can only be "critique" conceives metaphysics as being about the inside of our own heads, instead of being about the world. More recent anti-realists argue in the same vein that metaphysics is about our

29. Heil articulates this truth-maker principle in *Ontological Point of View*, p. 9.

30. See Thomas Reid, *Essays on the Intellectual Powers of Man*; G. E. Moore, *Proof of an External World*; J. L. Austin, *Sense and Sensibilia*. Selections from these works are all reprinted in Huemer, *Epistemology*.

concepts, or about our language.[31] There is something peculiarly baffling and self-defeating about this suggestion. Our concepts can have no content, and our words can have no meaning, other than by signifying things in the external world. Accordingly, we cannot coherently study language, or the structure of our own concepts, without simultaneously investigating the nature of external reality.

A Suggestion

Schopenhauer, like Kant, was writing under the illusion that physics was finished, that Newton's laws were the final word. Since the development of relativity theory and quantum mechanics, there is much less reason to think that science ever achieves certainty, or that any concept (including space, time, and causation) is immune to revision. The leading view nowadays in epistemology and philosophy of science is that, yes, what lies behind the empirical data is a riddle, but we answer that riddle in terms of an ever-evolving "web of belief." Any strand in that web might have to be destroyed, in the face of new data and creative new explanatory theories. At any given point in history, we have to pretend we know a good deal (in order to be comfortable in the world and in order to have the necessary background for research), but there is no guarantee that the whole general framework or worldview we accept will not be overthrown at some later time.[32]

I suggest we adopt such a view and that from now on we leave Schopenhauer's transcendental idealism aside. Let us treat Schopenhauer as if he were a creative scientist-cum-metaphysician,

31. An example of such a contemporary anti-realist is Michael Dummett, who seems to derive his anti-realism from extreme empiricism of the logical-positivist sort. See Dummett, *The Logical Basis of Metaphysics* (London: Duckworth, 1991).

32. This general view of our epistemic situation has been defended by W. V. O. Quine and Thomas S. Kuhn, among others. See Quine, "Two Dogmas of Empiricism," in *From a Logical Point of View* (Cambridge: Harvard University Press, 1953); Quine and J. S. Ullian, *The Web of Belief* (New York: Random House, 1970); and Kuhn, *The Essential Tension: Selected Studies in Scientific Tradition and Change* (Chicago: University of Chicago Press, 1977). The "tension" to which Kuhn refers is between the scientific community's dogmatic certainty, during times of normal research, that much of what it believes true, and the eventual willingness, in times of scientific revolution, to let go of this dogmatic certainty and adopt a new framework.

spinning theories about the nature of the reality behind the appearances, without the Kantian insistence that this reality must line up with our a priori thought structures. This may be untrue to Schopenhauer in one sense, but I like to think that it is true to him in a deeper sense. The anti-Kantian Schopenhauer was the real kernel of the man.

Schopenhauer's Panpsychism and Its Philosophical Ancestry

Much that is appealing in Schopenhauer's philosophy pulls against his transcendental idealism. Schopenhauer's great teaching is that the thing-in-itself is the mental force we know in ourselves as *will.* If transcendental idealism were true, we should be unable to know anything at all about the nature of the thing-in-itself. Further, Schopenhauer insists that the great, undifferentiated Will "objectifies itself" at various "levels." These "levels of objectification" include physical/chemical, vegetable, and animal kinds. But this doctrine of the "Platonic Forms" is curiously at odds with transcendental idealism. Are these kinds (these basic forces of nature, as Schopenhauer sees them) *real*, or are they imposed on reality by the human mind? Schopenhauer seems more inclined toward their ultimate reality than toward their artificiality. One piece of evidence for this: he teaches that the great value of art lies in depicting the Forms, and art penetrates beyond appearances to reality itself. Schopenhauer also observes that the basic forces of nature, which are noumenal, are that which "first gives to causes their causality, i.e., the ability to act, and hence that by which the causes hold this ability merely in fee."[33] Here we have Schopenhauer admitting that the power to act is a feature of the thing-in-itself, not at all imposed on the world by the mind.

I have remarked that epistemologically Schopenhauer sometimes seems to be pulling away from Kant and to be reaching toward pragmatic empiricism (in his insistence that observation is the source of both scientific and metaphysical knowledge, with no clear line between the two). It could equally well be said that Schopenhauer pulls away from Kant and reaches back toward the rationalists, in

---

33. Schopenhauer, *On the Fourfold Root of the Principle of Sufficient Reason*, trans. E. F. J. Payne (La Salle, Ill.: Open Court Publishing, 1974), p. 67.

that he indulges in precisely the sorts of flights of metaphysical fancy Kant objected to in the rationalists. But who can clearly separate flights of metaphysical fancy from creative scientific hypotheses?

Suppose we adopt, as a creative scientific hypothesis, the notion that everything in reality is both matter and mind—a dual-aspect theory. Schopenhauer's idea that reality consists of a great Will (prerational, unconscious mind), manifesting itself as various natural kinds and as the individuals in space and time belonging to those kinds, is an intriguing and original version of such a dual-aspect theory. Such a theory has several metaphysical advantages. If we accept such a theory, we can understand how reality is individuated into this and that. Each substance or object is separate because it has its own causal powers (its own internal motivation). Because activity is necessarily temporal, and substances or objects are the things that act, reality carries time within it. Time no longer comes into being with the first eye that opens, but forms the substrate of every object or substance that preexists the eye. Mind–body interaction, so problematic for the substance dualism of Descartes, becomes a nonissue. We no longer have to explain how *will* (Freud called it "the original psychical quality")[34] arises out of inert matter, since no matter is really inert. We still have a mind–body problem of sorts, since it is unclear how consciousness arises out of unconscious will, but it is easier to imagine how consciousness might arise out of unconscious *will* than to imagine how an active, internal causal power such as *will* originates from inert matter.

What shall we call this dual-aspect theory? We could call it "animism," since it blurs the distinction between living and nonliving matter. Today, biologists tell us that life is differentiated from nonlife by various entropy-resistant activities, such as metabolism, self-repair, and self-replication. These are all features of what we might call "autonomous action," the apparent striving of the organism to keep itself and its kind in existence. Schopenhauer's dual-aspect theory says that all substances and objects possess just such autonomy. According to Schopenhauer, living creatures differ from nonliving creatures not in essence, but only in the complexity of their causal powers.

We could also call Schopenhauer's dual-aspect theory "panpsychism," since *will* is undoubtedly a mental force or substance, and

34. See Freud, *An Outline of Psycho-analysis*, trans. James Strachey (New York: W. W. Norton and Co., 1949), p. 14. Freud, of course, called the original, unconscious will "id."

probably (just as Freud believed) the original one, out of which all others, such as intentionality and consciousness, arise.

Such a view has been appealing since human beings first started to think along scientific or metaphysical lines. Consider Aristotle's understanding of reality. Aristotle takes substances to be combinations of matter and form. Form, for Aristotle, is not just shape, but function or principle of action. Everything is, in a way, alive, according to Aristotle. For example, each of the four elements (earth, water, air, and fire) has its own internal principle of action that defines it. Earth, being the heaviest element, wants to find its place at the center of the cosmos; hence, it falls downward toward the center of our planet (which Aristotle, reasonably at that time, took to be the central body around which all the heavenly bodies revolved). Water, the second-heaviest element, seeks its place just above the earth; hence, water collects in oceans, lakes, and rivers on the surface of our world. Air, lighter than water, circulates above earth and water. Fire, lightest of all, leaps upward, seeking its place at the edge of the sublunary sphere.

Just as the nonliving elements possess internal principles of action that explain their motions, so do living creatures (which are, for Aristotle, the best examples of individual substances). Each organism inherently strives to nourish itself, to grow, to sense its environment, and to reproduce its kind.

Whereas we, in more modern times, attempt to explain the living world on the model of the nonliving world, Aristotle did the opposite. He took the mode of explanation we know "from the inside," motivational explanation, and applied it to everything.

Aristotle's view of things was so pleasingly intuitive that it was accepted in the Western world for many centuries. Even today, though we have officially thrown off Aristotle's chemistry and physics, we still can't help thinking along Aristotelian lines in biology (even when this seems to conflict with what modern biology tells us). However much we may pretend otherwise, it is impossible to understand the behavior of organisms without supposing they strive (consciously or unconsciously) toward self-preservation and preservation of their species.

Despite its intuitive appeal, the idea that substances and objects possess internal principles of action was officially rejected by the scientific community in the early-modern period. Aristotelian "substantial forms" became anathema, and a new way of thinking emerged. Reality consisted of inert material corpuscles. These corpuscles moved not because they wanted to, but because they were acted on by outside forces. This new way of thinking worked so well for falling bodies and orbiting planets that it became the ruling scientific orthodoxy to think that, eventually, it could be made to work for everything—chemicals, and even living things.

We are struggling even today with the problem of trying to fit life and mind into this paradigm. Though we have come to understand chemical reactions in terms of subatomic particles and the forces governing the structure of atoms, it is extremely difficult to understand human behavior, or the behavior of nonhuman animals, or even of plants, in this model. Life, with its purposeful, entropy-resistant activities such as metabolism, self-repair, and self-replication, is apparently a complex chemical phenomenon, but even modern scientists remain stumped as to how exactly living matter arises out of nonliving matter.[35]

If we look back at the history of early-modern philosophy, we see that the most acute of the scientist/philosophers of that era were aware that the hypothesis of inert matter acted on by outside forces was inadequate to account for the behavior of living systems. Aristotelianism never really died, it just went underground.

Leibniz was deeply sympathetic to the idea of internal principles of action within matter. In other words, Leibniz was the lone voice holding out for something like Aristotelian substantial forms. Without such a "living force" within matter, Leibniz thought, it would be impossible to know which of two bodies was moving:

> For if we consider only what motion contains precisely and formally, that is, change of place, motion is not something entirely real, and when several bodies change position among themselves, it is not possible to determine, merely from a consideration of these changes, to

---

35. Physicist Paul Davies writes, "[W]e have a good idea of the where and the when of life's origin, but we are a very long way from comprehending the how. This gulf in understanding is not merely ignorance about certain technical details, it is a major conceptual lacuna....[W]e are missing something very fundamental about the whole business." *The 5th Miracle: The Search for the Origin and Meaning of Life* (New York: Simon and Schuster, 1999), p. 17. Contrary to this statement, I believe the problem is that we just don't yet know all the (very complex) details. My idea is that there is really no major conceptual gap between life and nonlife at all. Rather, living things differ from nonliving things only in the complexity of their causal powers. Davies comes close to admitting this when he says, on p. 36 of the same work, "It is a mistake to seek a sharp dividing line between living and nonliving systems."

which body we should attribute motion or rest...but the force or proximate cause of these changes is something more real, and there is sufficient basis to attribute it to one body more than to another. Also, it is only in this way that we can know to which body the motion belongs. Now, this force is something different from size, shape, and motion, and one can therefore judge that not everything conceived in body consists solely in extension and in its modifications, as our moderns have convinced themselves. Thus we are...obliged to re-establish some beings or forms they have banished.[36]

Leibniz's main point in this passage is that you could have two worlds, in one of which A moves and B is stationary, and in the other of which B moves and A is stationary. But these facts cannot be distinguished unless the bodies are located in absolute space. The appeal to Aristotelian substantial forms, in order to explain motion, is mysterious.

Leibniz's entire metaphysical system is deeply mysterious and probably not entirely self-consistent. However, it contains some tantalizing suggestions. Leibniz was apparently struck by the fact that two attributes of living beings, perception and action, are impossible to explain given the early-modern hypothesis of mindless atoms moving in the void of space. He was forced to adopt the notion that the basic components of the cosmos are what he calls "monads," centers of perception and appetition. Though the great majority of the perceptions of most monads are unconscious, Leibniz thinks, some monads achieve consciousness. The world of matter described by physics, according to Leibniz, may be a "mere phenomenon," like the rainbow.[37] This phenomenal world can be understood as operating blindly according to Newtonian laws, but it can equally well be understood as operating according to teleological principles; the two systems of explanation are not in conflict, but rather are parallel and harmonious with each other.

Leibniz's great contemporary, Newton, never (to my knowledge) declared publicly that he was suspicious of inert matter, but he did spend much of his later life immersed in alchemy, fascinated by the "personalities" of the elements. Perhaps he, too, privately suspected that something like panpsychism might, after all, be true.

36. Leibniz, *Discourse on Metaphysics*, sec. 18.
37. Leibniz, letter to Antoine Arnauld, November 28/December 8, 1686. Reprinted in Roger Ariew and Eric Watkins, eds., *Modern Philosophy: An Anthology of Primary Sources* (Indianapolis: Hackett, 1998), pp. 214–217. The quoted passage about the rainbow occurs on p. 216.

The most straightforward, and the best-known, of early-modern dual-aspect theories is Spinoza's. The majestic metaphysics of Spinoza begins with the proposal that there is only one substance. Spinoza calls the one substance "God," though it bears no resemblance to the personal God of traditional Judeo-Christian religion. God is both thinking and extended. Instead of making mind and matter two substances, as Descartes (officially) had, Spinoza makes them two attributes of the same substance.[38] An attribute, he says, is a way of understanding the essence of the one substance. Thus, we may understand the universe to be essentially a thinking thing, or we may understand the universe to be essentially an extended thing. Either way of understanding reality is equally correct (and equally incorrect, since God actually has an infinity of attributes).

Within Spinoza's system, mind–body interaction becomes a non-issue. The one substance does what it does, and you can see these unfoldings either as the causal interactions of matter or as the volitional and rational progression of thought; it makes no difference. Every individual thing (every "mode of God," in Spinoza's terminology) is both a physical object and a mind or soul (an "idea," in Spinoza's terminology, which is in this case somewhat confusing). As Spinoza puts it, "All things are animate, though in different degrees."[39]

Talk of modes is talk of "particularized" properties, that is, properties that are not universals. Nowadays, philosophers (unaccountably) call these "tropes." For Spinoza, ordinary objects (trees, people, electrons) are not substances but modes or tropes—thickenings of the One, or ripples in the One. (Think of physical motion as like a horse wrinkling its skin to ward off flies.) On the corpuscularean view, too, ordinary objects are modes, not substances. They are ways the corpuscles are organized. The corpuscles are the only real substances.

There are obvious similarities between Spinoza's metaphysics and Schopenhauer's. Both take the entire universe to be animate. Both take all events to follow from preceding events with necessity. Both are struck by the suffering caused by our desiring nature and the indifference of the universe to humankind. Both recommend quieting the passions as a means of salvation.

38. The obvious question: How are these two attributes related? The surprising answer seems to be that they are *strictly identical*.
39. Spinoza, *Ethics*, pt. II, "Of the Nature and Origin of the Mind," prop. 13, note.

Of course, Spinoza is resolutely optimistic, whereas Schopenhauer is pessimistic. The deep difference really dividing the two is that Spinoza sees the universe as rational and neither good nor bad, whereas Schopenhauer sees it as irrational and bad.

Let us focus, however, on the panpsychism that Spinoza and Schopenhauer share. Such panpsychism is, in essence, the notion that all reality contains within itself a kind of drive, toward activity, toward ever greater complexity, and eventually toward consciousness.

Objections to Panpsychism Considered

The most obvious objection to such animism or panpsychism is that it is crazy because there is no evidence for it. Consider the brick serving as a doorstop in the corner. Obviously, it will be said, it isn't alive, and it has no mind. It isn't perceiving or willing anything, either consciously or unconsciously. It's just sitting there, and no amount of stimulation will make it do anything else.

Ah, but the brick is made of chemicals, and those chemicals possess their own internal proclivities to interact with other chemicals. If we threw the brick into the appropriate solution, it would dissolve, for example. We could say that the brick unconsciously perceives those substances with which it is able to interact, and fails to perceive the others. We could even say that the brick is "about" those other substances—its internal states have their own "physical intentionality."[40] Last and most important, we could say that the active causal powers of the chemicals making up the brick are the same thing we know in ourselves as *will*.

This sounds fanciful, but one could say that such panpsychism has exactly the same evidence in its favor as its materialist rival. Panpsychism and materialism are two different theories proposed to account for the same data, two different interpretations of the same observable facts. The situation between panpsychism and materialism resembles the standoff between psychological egoism and its rival proposal that people do sometimes act on altruistic motives.

40. The idea that intentionality or "aboutness" is ubiquitous, that physical states of nonliving systems are "about" their disposition-partners in causal interactions, has been defended by George Molnar. See his book *Powers: A Study in Metaphysics* (Oxford: Oxford University Press, 2003), pp. 61–66.

Motives, and causal powers in general, are unobservable. All we may observe are their effects (actions and movements).

Hypotheses may be attractive for their explanatory power, even when they do not suggest obvious modes of testing them against observable evidence. They may be attractive in this respect even when they lack another scientific virtue, an associated research program (fruitfulness in terms of presenting questions that may be investigated empirically). Panpsychism, like certain other hypotheses (here I think of some aspects of Freudian psychoanalysis, and the theory of "intelligent design"), has explanatory power without exhibiting some of the other virtues we might ideally want scientific hypotheses to have. If you like, you can say this makes it more metaphysical than scientific, but this does not mean it is either empty of content, or false.

Besides the "no-evidence" objection just discussed, I can think of another objection to panpsychism, which I call "the dead rabbit objection." In an attempt to reduce panpsychism to absurdity, an objector might say, "All right, according to you and Spinoza and Schopenhauer, everything is alive, only in different degrees. But that's crazy. It implies that a dead rabbit is not really dead; it's only less alive than a live rabbit. But, clearly, there is a definite line between life and death."

Clearly, when a living creature dies, something significant happens. One way of describing what happens is this: it ceases to exist as an object in its own right, and becomes a mere collection of other objects. What makes a rabbit a rabbit is a certain set of causal powers, and when the rabbit dies, it ceases to have those causal powers. A dead rabbit is not really a rabbit; it is a mere collection of decaying bone, hair, muscle, and other tissues. Indeed, in virtue of being dead and decaying, these tissues are not really tissues anymore; they have become masses of chemicals, reverting to what chemicals do when they are not part of living organisms. When the panpsychist asserts that these chemicals are alive in some degree, what he means is that chemicals possess their own intrinsic causal powers; they do something in virtue of their own nature. As to their possession of some rudimentary degree of perception—well, there is indeed no evidence of this except their reactivity. But what evidence have we that anything (besides ourselves) perceives, aside from its reactivity?

Many seventeenth- and eighteenth-century corpuscularians held that the corpuscles had intrinsic causal powers (e.g., Locke, Priestley). It may seem highly tendentious to characterize such a view as pan*psych*ism. Why, it will be asked, is causal power necessarily *mental* in nature? Why not assume instead that causal power is *physical*?

Why not, alternatively, take the line endorsed by Spinoza in the seventeenth century, and by Donald Davidson in the twentieth century, that the mental/physical dichotomy is not ontologically deep?[41] This is really the view I want to attribute to Schopenhauer—a dual-aspect theory or "neutral monism" according to which every individual thing is both a force (will) and a physical object. Perhaps it is misleading to call this view "panpsychism." But why not call it "panpsychism"? Everybody seems happy to call Spinoza a panpsychist.

Causal Power as Metaphysically Basic

One of the features that separates living from nonliving matter, we are told, is "autonomous" activity. Thus, Paul Davies writes:

> As a physicist, I am used to thinking of matter as passive, inert and clodlike, responding only when coerced by external forces—as when the dead bird plunges to the ground under the tug of gravity. But living creatures literally have a life of their own. It is as if they contain some inner spark that gives them autonomy, so that they can (within limits) do as they please. Even bacteria do their own thing in a restricted way. Does this inner freedom, this spontaneity, imply that life defies the laws of physics, or do organisms merely harness those laws for their own ends? If so, how? And where do such "ends" come from in a world apparently ruled by blind and purposeless forces?[42]

What do we mean, however, when we say that living things exhibit "autonomy," and in what respects is this really different from the properties of nonliving things, such as inorganic molecules? It is common to say that living things act, whereas nonliving things only react. However, as all determinist philosophers have noted, the

41. See Donald Davidson, "Mental Events," in *Essays on Actions and Events* (Oxford: Clarendon Press, 1980), pp. 207–227. According to Davidson, any event is a mental event if it can be picked out using mentalistic vocabulary. This, in effect, turns *all* events into mental events, but this result is not particularly metaphysically momentous.

42. Davies, *The 5th Miracle*, p. 33.

actions of living things are at bottom complex reactions to environmental stimuli. Nothing does anything without some triggering cause (except, perhaps, for quantum events, e.g., the spontaneous decay of a particle). Toss a piece of sodium into water, and you get an explosion. Present a hungry horse with a carrot, and you get eating behavior. One is just as caused as the other.

As I have said already, I agree with Fred Dretske that our talk of causation is through-and-through ambiguous between two notions, the above-mentioned "triggering cause" (the eliciting environmental stimulus) and "structuring cause," which I believe is most usefully understood as the nature of the substance(s) involved. As Dretske puts it, specifying the triggering cause explains why x happens now; specifying the structuring cause explains why x happens as opposed to y.[43] The explosion occurs (now) because you tossed the sodium into water. You get an explosion, as opposed to some other event, because of the natures (the molecular structures) of sodium and water. The eating behavior occurs (now) because you presented the hungry horse with a carrot. You get eating behavior, as opposed to some other event, because of the natures of horses and carrots, and the natural affinity between those two natures.

There is no deep sense in which the horse's behavior is "autonomous" and the sodium's behavior is not. All events have their causes. There is no "free will" in the sense of an event occurring without its dual explanation in terms of triggering and structuring causes (at least if we leave aside quantum mechanics, as I propose to do for the moment). So have determinist philosophers taught, and I find myself compelled to agree.

It has recently been suggested, by metaphysicians Heil, C. B. Martin, and George Molnar, that reality consists of objects and properties, and the properties of physical objects are just causal powers. Physical objects are individuated by their causal powers. Such causal powers are the internal natures of these objects, which endow them with the dispositions to react to certain other objects, should those objects become present in the environment.[44] Physical

43. Fred Dretske, *Explaining Behavior: Reasons in a World of Causes* (Cambridge: MIT Press, 1988), p. 42. As I noted in chapter 1 (p. 7, n. 11), Dretske describes structuring causes in terms of events. I think he should have said that structuring causes may be, and typically are, substances.

44. See Heil, *Ontological Point of View*, and works by C. B. Martin cited in Heil. See also C. B. Martin, *The Mind in Nature* (New York: Oxford University Press, 2007). Another proponent of this kind of view was the late George Molnar (see his

objects exist in a "power net" of mutual dispositions.[45] This proposal may seem hideously retrograde, a return to Aristotelianism in a scientific culture that has long since abandoned it. However, as noted above, I don't think Aristotle ever really died, and maybe it is time to take him out of the closet. I find the Heil/Martin/Molnar proposal plausible, and quite congenial to the kind of panpsychism I take Schopenhauer to have endorsed. Recall Schopenhauer's central thesis that motivation is causality seen from within. This, I believe, is the true solution to the mind–body problem. There is no special problem about so-called mental causation, because (in a deep sense) all causation is mental causation. The objects we officially describe as having minds differ from other objects only in the complexity of their causal powers.

As a philosophy of mind, this position (that mental properties are just a species of causal power) sounds like logical behaviorism, or maybe functionalism. It will be objected, of course, that such a position "leaves out the mind" by not considering subjectivity, consciousness, and qualia to be essential to what we mean by "mental." In reply, I can say that "mental" appears to be a cluster concept, and I do not consider consciousness and qualia to be essential to the mental. I certainly believe that there are unconscious mental states, and mental states that are nonqualitative (e.g., propositional attitudes). We count such states as mental primarily because of their causal (motivational) power. Subjectivity, perhaps, has some claim to be the essence of the mental, but for all we know, everything has a subjective aspect. (How would you know, unless you had been that thing?)

In a way, I am agreeing with Leibniz that the basic qualities of real objects are perception (which may be conscious or unconscious) and appetition (which, again, may be conscious or unconscious). This seems to me like another way of saying that real objects are differentiated by their causal powers and exist in a "power net" of mutual dispositions. Leibniz was simply considering causation "from the inside" rather than "from the outside." Leibniz's view

---

Powers). An earlier defender of the idea that properties are causal powers is Sydney Shoemaker; see his "Causality and Properties," reprinted in Tim Crane and Katalin Farkas, eds., *Metaphysics: A Guide and Anthology* (Oxford: Oxford University Press, 2004), pp. 273–295. It is important to note that there may be objects that are not physical objects: abstract objects such as numbers, propositions, and so forth. The properties of such abstract objects (oddness, evenness, primeness, truth, falsity, etc.) would not be causal powers.

45. "Power net" is C. B. Martin's term.

about causation is notoriously strange, since he officially denied that there was any such thing as causal power, asserting instead parallelism among monads. But if Schopenhauer is correct (and I think Spinoza had the same idea as Schopenhauer), then causation is not only real, but also more than we know—causation *is* both perception and appetition, seen from outside.

Determinism and Responsibility

Along with transcendental idealism and the panpsychist metaphysics of will, Schopenhauer's determinism surely deserves to be called a major theme. Once again, we see a kinship between Schopenhauer and Spinoza. Both envision a universe in which everything happens of necessity and we speak of contingency only because of our ignorance of the causes of events. Both declare that the notion of "free will," in the sense that the individual self could be the originating cause of an action, undetermined by causal factors extending beyond the self, makes no sense.

There are differences, however. Spinoza concludes that miserable human emotions such as guilt, regret, and remorse are useless and counterproductive. All such emotions can do is diminish one's current power of action and thought; therefore, we would be better off without them. In Spinoza's opinion, if you do something bad, the best reaction is to learn from it, move on, and don't do anything similar again. Repentance (being sorry you did it) is not a virtue, since it decreases your power of activity; further, it is stupid, since you should understand that you could not have done otherwise.[46]

Schopenhauer's opinion with regard to guilt and remorse appears to be somewhat different. He implies that it is natural to feel a deep sense of responsibility, since "I am the doer of my deeds" is an inescapable truth. One cannot change one's character, but one is nevertheless responsible for one's character, because this character *is* the self from which one's deeds proceed necessarily.[47] In some

46. See, e.g., Spinoza, *Ethics*, pt. IV, "Of Human Bondage," prop. 54: "Repentance is not a virtue, or does not arise from reason; but he who repents of an action is doubly wretched or infirm."

47. Schopenhauer, *Prize Essay on the Freedom of the Will*, trans. E. F. J. Payne, ed. Gunter Zoller (Cambridge: Cambridge University Press, 1999), pt. V, conclusion and higher view.

sense, Schopenhauer seems to approve of the Judeo-Christian sense of pervasive guilt. According to Schopenhauer, existence itself is the "original sin," since by existing we are doomed to participate in the cycle of destruction and suffering. Judaism and Christianity disguise this great truth beneath layers of myth, whereas the religions of India are more forthright about it, but the teaching that we are all "sinners" remains true. Hence, an attitude of happy guiltlessness is inappropriate.[48] This difference in moral attitude seems to reflect a difference in temperament. As previously noted, Spinoza was an action-oriented optimist, whereas Schopenhauer was rumination-prone pessimist.

Another difference, of course, is that Schopenhauer's determinism is supplemented by the notion that the individual self, as a unique manifestation of the thing-in-itself, has a noumenal aspect (the "intelligible character") that is outside space, time, and causality, and therefore transcendentally free.[49] Spinoza's only notion of freedom is acting in accordance with reason, spurred on by "active emotions" rather than "passive emotions."[50]

Neither of these notions of freedom allows a person to escape from the fact of determinism: any given action is the necessary result of prior causes, so the actor could not have done otherwise (not unless something about the situation had been different, or the actor had been a different person).

The current debate over free will divides theorists into "compatibilists" and "incompatibilists." The difference is over what is required for moral responsibility and whether this is compatible with determinism. Compatibilists believe that moral responsibility does not require the agent to be the originating cause of his action, nor does moral responsibility require that the agent "could have done otherwise" in the robust, nonhypothetical sense. All that is required for moral responsibility, according to the compatibilist, is that the agent's own character and desires are the proximate cause of his action, and that none of various excusing conditions (force, nonculpable ignorance, insanity, etc.) apply. All moral responsibility requires is that the agent be able to do what he (rationally) *wills*. Thus, according to compatibilism, the young gang-banger

48. See *WWR*, vol. 1, pp. 328–329, 354–355.
49. Schopenhauer, *Prize Essay*, pt. V, conclusion and higher view.
50. See Spinoza, *Ethics*, pts. IV and V. For examples of "active emotions," see pt. III, prop. 59, note.

who commits a robbery in order to obtain money to buy drugs is responsible for his action, despite the fact that his character and desires were shaped by the unfortunate and perverse subculture in which he found himself. As long as his rational will was basically in good working order (he wasn't psychotic) and as long as he was not forced by anyone else to do what he did, not suffering from any nonculpable mistake of fact, and so on, he is responsible.

Incompatibilists, by contrast, think that moral responsibility requires that the agent be the originating cause of his action. Not only must a moral agent be able to *do* what he *wills*, he must (somehow) have ultimate control over the content of his own will. Because the notion of an originating cause (an unmoved mover, sometimes referred to as an "agent cause") is seemingly impossible to fit into a scientific worldview, or even to make sense of, some incompatibilists have despaired of moral responsibility. One such contemporary philosopher, Derk Pereboom, calls himself a "hard incompatibilist" and argues that our moral and legal institutions should be free of retributive or punitive aspects, since people are never morally responsible for their actions.[51]

It is difficult to know how to classify Spinoza and Schopenhauer in these terms. Spinoza, perhaps, is a "hard incompatibilist" like Pereboom (though I think an equally strong case can be made that Spinoza is a compatibilist). But what about Schopenhauer? Is he a "hard incompatibilist," or some kind of compatibilist? Making this question even more difficult is the fact that Schopenhauer's view on free will is noticeably Kantian, and Kant is usually classified as a libertarian, a kind of incompatibilist who avows that we are originating causes of our actions and therefore morally responsible for them. Kant evidently thinks that the noumenal self (beyond space, time, and causality) is the origin of action and can be held responsible, even though the acts of the empirical self are as determined as everything else within the phenomenal world. To elaborate: Kant seems to think that the noumenal self (which is outside time) makes it the case that the world includes a causal chain that includes the free action. The self makes it the case that the world contains a particular structuring cause.[52] This is, to say the least, puzzling, and

---

51. See Derk Pereboom, *Living without Free Will* (Cambridge: Cambridge University Press, 2001).

52. A Kantian view of this kind on the free will problem is defended by E. J. Lowe in his *Subjects of Experience* (Cambridge: Cambridge University Press, 1996).

some of Schopenhauer's remarks, taken out of context, might sound like he agreed with it.

Schopenhauer states quite clearly, however, in his *Prize Essay on the Freedom of the Will*, that while he accepts Kant's distinction between the empirical character and the intelligible character, he does not accept the Kantian doctrine of noumenal responsibility. Discussing the apparent truth that a human being's actions have their determining ground in factors outside the person's own power, Schopenhauer says: "Kant attempts to clear up this great difficulty by means of the distinction between thing-in-itself and appearance; but it is so obvious that this does not alter the essence of the matter in any way that I am convinced he was not in earnest at all."[53]

There is a further striking difference between Schopenhauer's view and Kant's view in this area: Kant was a retributivist about criminal punishment, whereas Schopenhauer clearly thinks that criminal punishment is justified only by its deterrent effect.[54] Schopenhauer condemns retributivism in these words:

> All retaliation for wrong by inflicting a pain without any object for the future is revenge, and can have no other purpose than consolation for the suffering one has endured by the sight of the suffering one has caused in another. Such a thing is wickedness and cruelty, and cannot be ethically justified. Wrong inflicted on me by someone does not in any way entitle me to inflict wrong on him. Retaliation of evil for evil without any further purpose cannot be justified, either morally or otherwise, by any ground of reason, and the *jus talionis*, set up as an independent ultimate principle of the right to punish, is meaningless. Therefore, Kant's theory of punishment as mere requital for requital's sake is a thoroughly groundless and perverse view.[55]

It would be nice to think that Schopenhauer's considered view was not captured by the hackneyed compatibilist/incompatibilist distinction. Probably, Schopenhauer is best classified as a compatibilist, but perhaps it is not so important that we classify Schopenhauer's view as compatibilist or incompatibilist. What we can clearly understand about the view is the following: Schopenhauer believes that what we do in this world (the empirical world) is determined by

53. Schopenhauer, *Prize Essay*, p. 64. On p. 73 of the same work, Schopenhauer declares allegiance to the distinction between empirical and intelligible character.

54. See *WWR*, vol. I, p. 348.

55. *WWR*, vol. I, p. 348.

factors and events beyond our personal control. All events, including human actions, have causal explanations in terms of prior events, and these causal chains lead indefinitely back into the past. We are, in a sense, responsible for what we do, merely because we have done it (as the wind was responsible for the tree's falling on the house— causally responsible), but this does not imply that we could have done otherwise. Only another person could have done otherwise in the same circumstances. Our situation as actors in a deterministic world justifies compassion toward those who do wrong: "There, but for the grace of God, go I." Moral and legal sanctions are justified not because anybody really deserves punishment, but because the prospect of suffering such sanctions provides a causal factor, a motive, deterring at least some actors from antisocial conduct.

The topic of free will is an endlessly perplexing one, since it seems to be a necessary pragmatic presupposition of deliberation and action to imagine that we have open futures, that any of several different actions is possible for us at any given moment of choice. Yet, if determinism is true, open futures are an illusion; only one choice is really possible, and deliberation has an outcome already set by character and circumstances. To say to someone, "It's up to you," is curiously ambiguous. Are we telling him he actually has a radically free choice? Are we telling him that whatever choice he makes will reveal who he is, and can't help being? Are we simply saying that what he does depends on what he chooses, what course of action he settles on?

It often seems to me as if radical (noncompatibilist) free will were a "noble lie," a falsehood we ought to inculcate in our children because believing it will make them better people. The most intelligent among them will eventually figure out that it isn't true, but having believed it in their youth will have enabled them to reach their full potential. Throughout life, whatever our theoretical convictions, free will remains a necessary practical illusion.

Whatever the truth of these speculations, the notion that a given person, with a given character, at a given point in time, faced with a given set of circumstances, could choose any of several open options is dismissed by Schopenhauer as ridiculous. This would be *liberum arbitrium indifferentiae*, the denial of determinism, and here "clear thinking is at an end."[56] Such a thing would make human action utterly inexplicable, and everything in the phenomenal world must

56. Schopenhauer, *Prize Essay*, p. 8.

be explicable, reducible to some sort of necessary ground under the Principle of Sufficient Reason.

Quantum Mechanics

The vision of the universe shared by Schopenhauer and Spinoza is that of a great system, magisterially indifferent to human beings and their petty needs and concerns, within which everything happens necessarily. One objection I can no longer avoid facing is this: modern physics, apparently, has revealed that determinism isn't true. The most basic components of reality, subatomic quanta, behave according to laws, but these laws are probabilistic, not deterministic. Trying to explain everything in terms of deterministic laws is a relic of an outmoded worldview. Seeing the universe as a wholly deterministic system was possible for a person of the seventeenth, eighteenth, or nineteenth centuries, but is not possible for a well-informed person of today.

Albert Einstein, notoriously, resisted quantum mechanics until the end of his days, despite the fact that some of his own discoveries laid the groundwork for it. "God does not play dice with the universe," Einstein insisted. As is typical of important transitional thinkers, Einstein was caught with one foot in the new paradigm he helped forge, and the other foot (along with his heart) still in the old paradigm.[57]

Well, let us face the challenge: Does the fact that quantum-mechanical laws are probabilistic rather than deterministic undermine Schopenhauer's insistence that the Principle of Sufficient Reason governs events in the (macrolevel) phenomenal world? Not unless it can be shown that quantum indeterminacy "translates up"

---

57. Einstein apparently read, and admired, Schopenhauer's work on free will. Max Planck reported Einstein as saying, "Honestly I can't understand what people mean when they talk about the freedom of the will. I feel that I will to light my pipe, and I do it, but how can I connect this up with the idea of freedom? What is behind the act of willing to light the pipe? Another act of willing? Schopenhauer once said, 'Der Mensch kann was er will; er kann aber nicht wollen was er will.'" The translation of the quoted passage is, roughly, "Man can do what he wills, but he can't will what he wills." Reported in Sir James Jeans, *Physics and Philosophy* (New York: Dover, 1981), p. 213. This makes Schopenhauer look like a classical compatibilist, echoing Locke: actions are free if willed, and it makes no sense to ask if *willing* is free.

into the world of larger objects, and as far as I know, this has not been established. Scientific practice, so far, continues to insist on deterministic explanations in chemistry, biology, and so on. The idea that the laws of higher level sciences can be reduced to the laws of quantum mechanics remains a metaphysical dream, unrealized in practice. Perhaps the sort of emergence Schopenhauer favored is the truth—that is, novel and unpredictable causal powers appear at different ontological levels. If this were true, then the causal powers of chemical elements would not be wholly explicable in terms of quantum mechanical laws, and the causal powers of biological systems would not be wholly explicable in terms of chemistry. This is mysterious, but it may be the way the world is.

With regard to the free will problem, some people seem to think that undetermined quantum events in the brain might confer on human beings the "free will" we desire, but this is puzzling for the following reason: How could I be responsible for an act that just happened, caused neither by my character nor by anything else?

There are other features of quantum mechanics to consider besides the fact that its laws are nondeterministic, and some of those features would actually please Schopenhauer, since they suggest that some sort of idealism may be true. (Alas for me and my anti-idealist prejudices!)[58]

The results of well-known experiments reveal that photons and electrons act like waves when there are no detectors present, but act like particles in the presence of detectors.[59] According to the standard interpretation of quantum mechanics (known as "the

58. My description of the results of quantum experiments, and the interpretation thereof, is necessarily brief, but I hope it is not inaccurate. The following books have taught me what I know about quantum theory: Werner Heisenberg, *Physics and Philosophy: The Revolution in Modern Science* (Amherst, N.Y.: Prometheus Books, 1999); Heinz R. Pagels, *The Cosmic Code: Quantum Physics as the Language of Nature* (Toronto: Bantam Books, 1982); Nick Herbert, *Quantum Reality: Beyond the New Physics* (New York: Doubleday, 1985); and James T. Cushing, *Philosophical Concepts in Physics* (Cambridge: Cambridge University Press, 1998). I have also been helped by innumerable conversations with my friend physicist George Patsakos.

59. A clear description of these "two slit" and "beam splitter" experiments is provided by Richard DeWitt in *Worldviews: An Introduction to the History and Philosophy of Science* (Oxford: Blackwell, 2004), chap. 25. In general, DeWitt's book contains the clearest and most teachable treatment of quantum theory I know of for nonphysicists. However, it is worth noting that the standard account of the results of quantum experiments requires us to consider *detectors* as somehow outside the system. If quantum theory is the whole story, this makes no sense. In fact, this

Copenhagen interpretation," since Werner Heisenberg and Niels Bohr came up with it in Copenhagen), quanta do not have any particular characteristics (e.g., position, velocity, and spin) until we measure them. Somehow (don't ask how) our acts of measurement bring definite facts into existence; prior to measurement, there are just probabilities.

Einstein disliked the idea that things could exist without having definite characteristics. Along with Erwin Schrodinger, Einstein believed there had to be "hidden variables"—that is, quantum entities must have definite characteristics even when we are not measuring them. In 1935, Einstein and his colleagues Rosen and Podolsky made up a thought experiment (known as the EPR thought experiment) to prove their point of view. The result of the EPR thought experiment is this: either quanta must have definite characteristics prior to measurement, or there must be influences that travel faster than light (what Einstein refused to believe in, and called "spooky action at a distance").

David Bohm actually formulated a version of quantum theory with "hidden variables," that is, a theory in which the quanta have definite characteristics prior to measurement. Unfortunately, Bohm's theory also involved faster-than-light influences (the spooky thing Einstein eschewed). This was no accident, as John Bell later proved. Bell, in the 1960s, proved a remarkable mathematical result that has come to be known as "Bell's theorem" or "the Bell inequality." Any system in which the objects being measured have definite characteristics prior to measurement, and in which there are no faster-than-light influences, must conform to the Bell inequality; this is what Bell proved. An EPR-type quantum experiment involving polarized photons and polarization detectors, however, violates the Bell inequality. This indicates that in quantum reality, either there are no "hidden variables," or there is "spooky action at a distance." (Take your pick of weirdness!)

I do not know what to make of the strangeness of quantum theory. Fortunately for me, neither does anybody else. What we have is an excellent theory, but no clear conception of what the world must be like if that theory is true. We grasp the theory, but not its truth makers. Maybe we should conclude that quantum physics makes bad metaphysics.

---

interpretation of quantum experiments is epistemically loaded, a manifestation of latent verificationism among physicists.

It seems that somehow, a world governed by familiar, classical, deterministic laws emerges out of the quantum world. Nobody understands this, but it appears to be the way it is. As long as we continue to operate according to the Principle of Sufficient Reason at the level of ordinary, middle-sized objects, I will hold out for Schopenhauer's views on freedom and determinism.

CHAPTER THREE

Schopenhauer's Anti-Kantian Account of Morality

Kantian Ethics: Its Appeal and Its Puzzling Aspects

The key idea of Kant's ethical theory is that the "maxim" of one's act (the rule upon which one implicitly acts) must be *universalizable*: it should be possible, without contradiction, to will that everyone, in a similar situation, should act the same as you. If one acts on a maxim that is *not* universalizable, one is guilty of internal incoherence and has failed in terms of rationality.

Kant's appeal to universalizability is undoubtedly attractive. All of us remember our mothers asking us, "What if everyone did that?" when we committed some moral transgression. This rhetorical question embodies a general principle something like this: if you wouldn't want everyone else to act in a certain way, then you shouldn't act in that way yourself.[1] Well, *why* wouldn't you want everyone else to act in that way? Maybe because it would have bad consequences in general, or because (egoistically) you wouldn't want others to treat you as you are contemplating treating others. Kant, however, thinks there are deeper reasons why the maxim of an action must be universalizable, having to do with the internal reasonableness of the agent. If you act on a nonuniversalizable maxim,

---

1. See Fred Feldman, "An Examination of Kantian Ethics," in Louis P. Pojman, ed., *Moral Philosophy: A Reader*, 3rd ed. (Indianapolis: Hackett, 2003), p. 214.

says Kant, you literally contradict yourself—you simultaneously will two opposing actions. Even if Kant is wrong about this, we can at least see the intuitive appeal of the basic idea.

Another admittedly attractive aspect of Kantian ethics is Kant's insistence that a rational agent is capable, sometimes, of performing an action that goes against (many of) her inclinations, simply because it is the right thing to do. Sometimes the right action will not make anybody happy, but one is morally required to do it anyway. The ability to act against many strong inclinations, on moral principle, is unique to rational beings. Kant teaches that this unique, awe-inspiring ability constitutes grounds for respecting rational beings. All this has intuitive appeal.

Nevertheless, one might suspect that Kant's project is doomed at the start, due to presupposing a false account of human psychological structure. Kant is trying to argue that reason itself can motivate action, without any admixture of desire or other emotional incentive. Many thinkers have concluded that human beings do not work that way. Hume, for example, asserted that reason is the slave of the passions,[2] and Spinoza implied that mere understanding, without emotion, cannot motivate action, because humans are, essentially, desiring creatures.[3] Even Kant, who thinks there are (or at least ought to be) counterexamples to the notion that all action is motivated by desire, admits that since the "inner principle" of action is invisible, it is impossible by means of experience to tell whether an action is motivated by emotion or by pure reason.[4] If Hume and Spinoza are

2. Hume, *A Treatise of Human Nature*, bk. 2, pt. III, sec. 3, "Of the Influencing Motives of the Will": "I shall endeavor to prove, *first*, that reason alone can never be a motive to any action of the will; and *secondly*, that it can never oppose passion in the direction of the will." Hume goes on, later in the same section, to make the famous remark, "Reason is, and ought only to be the slave of the passions, and can never pretend to any other office than to serve and obey them."

3. According to Spinoza, the very essence of a thing is emotional—its desire or striving to keep itself in existence (*Ethics*, pt. III, "Of the Origin and Nature of the Emotions," props. 6, 7). Spinoza teaches that there are two kinds of emotions, passive (based on obscure and confused ideas) and active (based on clear and distinct ideas) (*Ethics*, pt. III, props. 58, 59). Passive emotions motivate the sorts of behavior Spinoza calls "human bondage"—compulsive and addictive behaviors, and other foolish behaviors contrary to the real interests of the person. Active emotions motivate the sorts of behaviors genuinely in the creature's self-interest. It seems to be implied here that both kinds of behavior are emotionally directed, rather than originating in pure reason.

4. Kant, *Foundations of the Metaphysics of Morals*, trans. Lewis White Beck (Indianapolis: Bobbs-Merrill, 1959), p. 23.

correct, and desire lies behind every action, the Kantian idea of a categorical imperative is an absurdity. (Schopenhauer would call it an "iron-wood.") All imperatives are necessarily hypothetical.

Of course, among the desires of any well-socialized, nonpsychopathic human being is the desire to do the right thing. But what is the right thing? It's not like we can just consult pure reason and find out some nonambiguous answer. Our actual situation, as moral agents, is well described by the deontological moral intuitionist W. D. Ross: we find ourselves, in any morally significant situation, with many competing prima facie duties.[5] Each of these prima facie duties pulls or inclines us in some direction or other. We have duties of fidelity, based on past promises, explicit or implicit. We have duties of reparation and gratitude, based on past acts of ourselves and others. We have duties of justice (duties to see that benefits and burdens are distributed fairly). We have duties of nonmaleficence (to avoid doing harm) and duties of beneficence (to help others when we can). We also have duties to ourselves, to pursue our own self-interest and to improve ourselves and our situation. When these prima facie duties conflict with each other, as they almost always do, we must, eventually, choose among them and act. In the end, we go with whichever duty seems to us most weighty. But such choices are never clear, and we are seldom free of uncertainty and regret. This is the nature of the moral life. We choose, and act, in fear and trembling, ever unsure that what we do is really the right thing, all things considered.

Kant, however, has a very different vision both of the nature of a human being and of the moral situation. Human beings, uniquely among animals, possess self-consciousness and the capacity to deliberate about their actions. Why? Here, Kant isn't asking why consciousness and deliberation evolved, since he is writing prior to the advent of Darwinian theory. Instead, he is pretty clearly thinking in theological terms: Why would God have given to human beings their peculiar, conscious, deliberative form of practical reason? If God intended human beings to behave just like other animals, seeking ends such as nutrition, growth, physical comfort, reproduction, and so on, why wouldn't God have made human beings so that they sought these ends instinctively? Why bother giving human beings

the capacity to question, which only interferes with their achievement of these natural kinds of happiness shared with other living
creatures? Kant concludes that God must have intended human
beings to devote their lives to a higher end, an end discernible only
by the activity of abstract reason. What is this end? Human beings,
Kant thinks, are intended not to pursue their own happiness, but
to do their duty. It is one of the paradoxes of human life that it is
only by devoting oneself to duty, and turning away from the pursuit of happiness, that one actually achieves the kind of happiness
peculiar to a human being, and of which a human being is uniquely
worthy.[6]

But what is the content of this duty, allegedly accessible to
abstract reason? There's the rub. Kant assumes that any person of
"natural sound understanding" can look into his or her own reason
and find there such duties as always treating others with fairness
(never cheating others). He mentions the shopkeeper who always
charges everybody the same, fair price, even ignorant persons he
might overcharge and get away with it. If the shopkeeper behaves
this way out of prudence or self-interest (it's good for business to
have a reputation for honesty), then, says Kant, his action has no
moral worth. The shopkeeper is behaving merely in accordance
with duty, but not from duty. Fair and honest action has moral
worth only when done because the actor realizes it is his duty and
does it because it is his duty. If doing his duty goes against his own
personal inclinations, so much the better for the moral worth of the
action. Actually wanting to be fair to others because one sympa-
thizes with them, Kant thinks, has no moral value whatsoever; it is
a mere inclination.

There are many things about this that puzzle me. What about
Kant's claim that there is a "don't cheat" rule written into the very
fabric of human reason? I am willing to grant that all cognitively
normal human beings seem to be endowed with moral intuitions
concerning fairness. We innately recognize when a distribution of
goods is unequal and the inequality is not justified by some relevant
difference in merit. Likewise, we innately recognize when the burdens of a cooperative venture are assigned unequally and there is
no justification for some people getting a greater share of the work

6. Aristotle says something like this, too—you won't find happiness (*eudaimonea*)
by aiming at happiness. Happiness comes as a side effect of aiming at other, more
specific ends—in particular, virtuous actions. See *Nicomachean Ethics*, bk. 1, chap. 9.

without a corresponding share of the profits. Yet, when we are lucky enough to be one of those who benefits from the unfairness, we are usually not prone to squeal. Typically, we squeal only when we suffer from unfair arrangements, not when we profit from them. In general, when social rules allow the "free rider" phenomenon (we can reap the benefits of most everyone else following the rule, and save ourselves inconvenience, by choosing not to follow the rules when nobody is looking), people can be counted on to be "free riders" and not to feel particularly guilty about it. Thus, we seem to have two sets of competing moral intuitions—self-interest and personal survival, on the one hand, versus the socially useful desire to be a good cooperator, on the other hand. It has been noticed that there are good evolutionary reasons for both sorts of moral intuitions to have spread widely in human populations. Self-interest and personal survival instincts make it more likely that one's genes will be present in future populations. Cooperative instincts make it more likely that one's social group will cohere, succeed, and be able to defeat other groups in the competition for resources. Thus, individual and group natural selection provide a plausible explanation for why these two kinds of competing moral intuitions are so typical of humankind. Indeed, the tension between the two kinds of moral intuition is typical of the moral life.[7] None of this, however, supports Kant's claim that there is an absolute "don't cheat" rule discernible by reason. The evidence, and its evolutionary explanation, supports only the claim that "don't cheat" is a prima facie duty, one that may be overridden by competing considerations.

What about Kant's notion that an action in accordance with fairness has no moral worth unless it is done "from duty" rather than from inclination, and that it gains in moral worth insofar as it is done against inclination? Kant makes this his First Proposition of Morality: "An act must be done from a sense of duty to have moral worth."[8] This doctrine is so strange I have great difficulty trying to see it from Kant's point of view so that it has any plausibility. My own intuition is that an action gains in moral worth by being done out of a sense of empathy or out of a genuine desire to be a good cooperator.

7. See Howard Kahane, "Sociobiology, Egoism, and Reciprocity," in Louis Pojman, ed., *Moral Philosophy: A Reader*, 3rd ed. (Indianapolis: Hackett, 2003), pp. 87–103.

8. Kant, *Foundations*, p. 16.

It is difficult to see where moral rules come from, if not from human moral intuitions, which are themselves inclinations. Take inclinations utterly out of the picture, and what are we left with? Perhaps it is true that a rational being is necessarily a rule-following being, but the content of the rules is nowhere given, except by what we may find ourselves wanting to accomplish or caring about. Rules without reference to ends are, literally, incomprehensible. Yet, this is ultimately Kant's notion of duty: a rule without reference to any end, a rule you simply have to follow because...why? Well, just because.

Kant goes on to declare that it is obviously a duty to preserve one's own life, even when one's life has become unbearably painful and sad and one can't think of anything that makes one's life worth living anymore and wants to die. Whereas it has no moral worth to preserve one's life when one is enjoying it, it has great moral worth to go on living when one is suicidally miserable. Why? Because duty commands it, and the only thing that has real moral worth is to act from duty, preferably against inclination.

I don't understand this. Who says it is a duty to go on living, no matter how miserable one's life is? I have quite the contrary intuition. Rational suicide seems quite possible to me. I defy anyone to explain to me why it is rational to go on living when one's life no longer offers the pleasures and accomplishments that once made it worth living, or when one is slowly losing one's autonomy and dignity due to a brain-destroying disease, or in any number of other tragic circumstances.[9]

The Second Proposition of Morality, according to Kant, is as follows:

> An action performed from duty does not have its moral worth in the purpose which is to be achieved through it but in the maxim by which it is determined. Its moral value, therefore, does not depend on the realization of the object of the action but merely on the

---

9. Incidentally, Schopenhauer condemns suicide, but on different grounds from Kant's. According to Schopenhauer, the ethical ideal is to *stop willing* altogether, to stop caring about, or desiring, the pleasures of one's individual existence. The person who commits suicide, Schopenhauer says, "wills life, and is dissatisfied merely with the conditions on which it has come to him." *The World as Will and Representation* (hereafter *WWR*), vol. 1, p. 398. Suicide, therefore, is a phenomenon of *affirmation* of the will. This makes it antithetical to the highest moral conduct, for Schopenhauer, since his moral ideal is denial of the will. This is one part of Schopenhauer's philosophy with which I cannot concur.

principle of volition by which the action is done, without any regard to the objects of the faculty of desire.[10]

This is a dense passage, and it is important to understand it correctly. Common sense and law agree that an agent's degree of moral responsibility for his action depends on his mental state when he performs the action. Doing a bad act intentionally is worse than doing it merely recklessly or negligently. A related point is that a person with no culpable mental state at all may perform a bad act. This is what happens when certain legitimate excusing conditions apply, such as force or nonculpable mistake of fact. In such cases, we do not hold the agent responsible. We evaluate the agent in terms of what was he was trying to do or what he wished (his mental state at the time of the act), not in terms of what actually comes about. But this is not what Kant means (or, at least, it is not all Kant means) when he says that the moral worth of an action depends on the "principle of volition by which the action is done."

Kant's notion of a "maxim" or "principle of volition" is tricky. He thinks that whenever a person wills an action, the person may be understood as following a rule. The rational *will*, for Kant, is precisely the faculty that acts in accordance with rules. Kant says that "the will stands, as it were, at a crossroads halfway between its a priori principle which is formal and its a posteriori incentive which is material."[11]

What does he mean? Apparently, Kant believes that a rational being is necessarily a rule-following being (and he seems right about that much). Therefore, the empty form of a rule must be represented in a priori reason, as a condition of rational action. However, where does a rule get its specific content? Kant's epistemology in general implies that while *form* is a priori, *content* is a posteriori. Therefore, exactly what rules to follow would have to be determined in some way by experience. Since we are dealing here with action rather than cognition, one would naturally think that the content of the rule would be derived from both experience and desire or inclination. But no. Kant continues: "Since [the will] must be determined by something, if [the action] is done from duty it must be determined by the formal principle of volition as such, since every material principle has been withdrawn from it."[12]

10. Kant, *Foundations*, p. 16.
11. Kant, *Foundations*, p. 16.
12. Kant, *Foundations*, p. 16.

The crucial idea of Kant's ethics is that an action done "from duty" or "out of respect for the law" (these seem to be alternative phrases expressing the same notion) is an action commanded by the very fact that rational action is necessarily rule governed. It is as if there were a metarule stating, "Whatever rule you follow in performing an action, it had better be a genuine *rule*." And Kant's idea of a genuine rule is an absolute rule, one that every rational being could follow in similar circumstances without creating any pragmatic contradiction. Thus we get the first formulation of the categorical imperative: "Act only according to that maxim by which you can at the same time will that it should become a universal law."[13]

The idea of a pragmatic contradiction is best illustrated by Kant's example of the lying promise to pay back a loan.[14] Suppose I borrow money, promising to pay it back, all the time knowing full well that I can't pay it back. According to Kant, the maxim of this action contains a pragmatic contradiction because, if everyone made promises intending to break them, the whole institution of promise keeping would crumble and, along with it, contract law, commerce, and so on. It is a presupposition of my making a promise that a promise is to be kept. So, if I make a promise intending to break it, I am undermining the very institution on which my action depends.

This makes a certain amount of sense. Still, it remains true that people do break promises, sometimes, yet the institution of promise keeping survives. Where's the contradiction? Making exceptions to a rule, sometimes, isn't really *contradictory*; it's just, well, messy, as human life and human institutions tend to be. Isn't it enough if to keep one's promises is a prima facie duty, rather than an absolute duty?

Kant's other attempts to illustrate the alleged contradictions involved in violating the categorical imperative are even less convincing than the lying-promise example. With regard to the fellow, mentioned above, who decides to commit suicide because he is miserable, Kant says:

> Now he asks whether the maxim of his action could become a universal law of nature. His maxim, however, is: For love of myself, I make it my principle to shorten my life when by a longer duration it threatens more evil than satisfaction. But it is questionable whether this principle of self-love could become a universal law of nature. One immediately sees a contradiction in a system of nature whose

13. Kant, *Foundations*, p. 39.
14. Kant, *Foundations*, p. 40.

law would be to destroy life by the feeling whose special office is to impel the improvement of life.[15]

Kant believes that self-love and desire for pleasure are intended by God or nature to preserve life, and so, when one commits suicide because one's life is no longer pleasant, one is turning the life instinct against itself. One is, as Kant would say, using oneself as a means to an end. Again, this makes a certain amount of sense; one can sort of see what Kant is getting at. Still, where is the actual contradiction? If people only committed suicide when they were miserable, when their lives no longer offered them any meaningful satisfactions, would the life instinct be utterly undermined? Of course not; life would go on (as it in fact does) since most people, most of the time, do find meaningful satisfactions in life.

Another of Kant's examples concerns the alleged duty to develop one's talents. I will use myself as an illustration this time. I have a talent for writing and a talent for singing (minor talents, perhaps, but still talents). These were gifts of nature with which I was born. However, suppose that instead of deciding to work at developing these gifts, I decide to neglect them and spend my time lying in the sun, drinking alcoholic beverages, and smoking marijuana (in Margaritaville, perhaps) instead of writing philosophy books and singing in choirs. Kant admits that a society could exist where everyone similarly wills not to develop their talents (he mentions "the South Sea Islanders," an example unfair to any actual South Sea tribes). However, oddly, he declares that if I made this decision, I would be contradicting myself: "For, as a rational being, [s]he necessarily wills that all [her] faculties should be developed."[16]

This is such a blatant example of question-begging that I am astonished anyone as smart as Kant would produce it. Precisely the question at issue is whether it is necessary that a rational being wills to develop her talents. An example has been produced suggesting that it is not necessary, but indeed quite possible, and probably quite common among human beings. Kant simply replies that it is necessary, without any argument at all.

I will grant, in agreement with John Stuart Mill (see his *Utilitarianism*) that people who choose not to develop their own talents are less happy overall than their counterparts who go on and

15. Kant, *Foundations*, pp. 39–40.
16. Kant, *Foundations*, p. 41.

exert the effort necessary to develop their natural abilities. There is a special, "higher" kind of pleasure that comes from doing the things one has a gift for, even though developing the gift can involve (along the road) a great deal of hard work, disappointment, humiliation, depression, and frustration. The satisfaction of doing something really excellent, finally, makes it all worthwhile. However, none of this changes the fact that there is no contradiction in willing not to develop one's talents. It is sad and disappointing, perhaps, when someone wills to squander his gifts, but not contradictory.

Perhaps Kant is thinking along these lines: everyone naturally desires achievement, excellence, and recognition, in addition to desiring leisure, recreation, and sensual pleasures. The person who chooses not to develop her talents, and devotes herself to leisure and sensual pleasure instead, will inevitably have a conflict within herself, because she knows that if she had made the necessary effort, she could have had the "higher pleasures" of excellence and achievement. Thus, it is typical that people who choose not to develop their talents are conflicted and tortured by self-loathing. Perhaps this is what Kant has in mind when he says they have a contradiction in their wills. However, this "contradiction," if you want to call it that, is *affective*; it is a conflict between two sorts of *desires*. It has nothing to do with being rationally unable to will that the maxim "choose leisure and sensual pleasure over arduous development of talents" should become a universal law. As far as I can see, willing this maxim to be a universal law would be perfectly consistent. It would show a preference for one kind of pleasure over another, that's all.

Kant's final example is that of a Scrooge-like man who decides not to help anyone else, but just to look after his own interests: "[This] man, for whom things are going well, sees that others (whom he could help) have to struggle with great hardships, and he asks, 'What concern of mine is it? Let each one be as happy as heaven wills, or as he can make himself; I will not take anything from him or even envy him; but to his welfare or to his assistance in time of need I have no desire to contribute.'"[17] Kant grants that a world could exist in which everyone thought and behaved like Scrooge, but he says it is nevertheless impossible to *will* the existence of such a world: "For a will which resolved this would conflict with

---

17. Kant, *Foundations*, p. 41.

itself, since instances can often arise in which he would need the love and sympathy of others, and in which he would have robbed himself, by such a law of nature springing from his own will, of all hope of the aid he desires."[18]

However, even if Scrooge may someday (if he becomes poor) will that someone else should help him, it doesn't follow that there's any contradiction in his will today, when he says, "Bah! Humbug!" to the idea of Christian charity. Besides, Scrooge might be absolutely consistent in his egoism, and even if he became poor, he might not will that anyone else should help him. He might say, "If I cannot help myself, so much the worse for me." So, again, where's the contradiction?

On the whole, then, none of Kant's examples is successful in showing that violating any of his alleged duties involves the agent in a pragmatic contradiction. One may suspect that the very notion of a categorical imperative is defective. A rule with no content cannot command anything in particular. Besides, who says any rule has to be absolute? Maybe all rules have exceptions.

Kant sees the great difficulty he is up against:

> [W]e are not yet advanced far enough to prove a priori that that kind of imperative really exists, that there is a practical law which of itself commands absolutely and without any incentives, and that obedience to this law is duty....Is it a necessary law for all rational beings that they should always judge their actions by such maxims as they themselves could will to serve as universal laws? If it is such a law, it must be connected (wholly a priori) with the concept of the will of a rational being as such. But in order to discover this connection we must, however reluctantly, take a step into metaphysics.... [I]f reason of itself alone determines conduct it must necessarily do so a priori. The possibility of reason thus determining conduct must now be investigated.[19]

Kant reasons, in a very obscure passage, to the conclusion that strictly speaking a "categorical imperative" *does* require an "end," something for the sake of which the law is obeyed. However, this "end" must be "something the existence of which in itself has absolute worth," or "an end in itself."[20] Kant thinks *rational beings* are such ends in themselves, because...? Here Kant's reasoning becomes

---

18. Kant, *Foundations*, p. 41.
19. Kant, *Foundations*, pp. 43–45.
20. Kant, *Foundations*, pp. 46–47.

especially hard to follow. He apparently thinks rational beings are ends in themselves because they are capable of overcoming inclination and acting in accordance with duty, which makes them worthy of respect. All this seems maddeningly circular and question-begging. None of these claims have been proven, and Kant keeps using these unsupported claims as support for each other. By this murky route Kant arrives at the second formulation of the categorical imperative: "Act so that you treat humanity, whether in your own person or in that of another, always as an end and never as a means only."[21] At this point in reading Kant's treatise, one feels that one has been subjected to an illusionist trick. A rabbit has been pulled out of a hat. Where did it come from?

Incidentally, some of Kant's remarks in this context are offensive to animal lovers, implying that *only* human beings have moral worth or are deserving of respect. Nonhuman animals, according to Kant, are mere "things," and we may use them for whatever ends we choose, with no moral qualms whatsoever, except insofar as ill treatment of animals might indirectly make us less sensitive to our duties toward humans.

There is a third formulation of the categorical imperative, which is rather hard to state, and which bears an obvious relationship to the first formulation. Here are a few of the sentences in which Kant struggles to express it:

> [I]n volition from duty the renunciation of all interest is the specific mark of the categorical imperative, distinguishing it from the hypothetical. And this is now being done in the third formulation of the principle, i.e., in the idea of the will of every rational being as a will giving universal law....Or, better: if there is a categorical imperative (a law for the will of every rational being), it can only command that everything be done from the maxim of its will as one which could have as its object only itself considered as giving universal laws.[22]

When a rational being acts according to universalizable maxims, Kant declares, his will is "autonomous" as opposed to "heteronomous." A heteronomous will is the normal sort of will that acts according to inclination and does not require that the maxims of its acts should be universal laws for all rational beings.

21. Kant, *Foundations*, p. 47.
22. Kant, *Foundations*, p. 50.

Perhaps the idea here is that we generally act on nonmoral norms (in ways that, we hope, are morally permissible). A *moral* action, however, is one that is not grounded in any contingent inclination, but in the nature of reason itself. (I have never been able to grasp the idea of such an action. I admit, I am a Humean with regard to motivation.)

Kant envisions all rational beings in the universe dwelling together in what he calls a "realm of ends." Rational beings, because they are capable of autonomy, are beyond all price, possess dignity, and are worthy of respect. (Again, this has the disturbing implication that nonhuman animals are outside the moral sphere, unworthy of respect, mere objects to be bought and sold, no different morally speaking from tables and chairs.)

I have a problem with Kant's notion of a "realm of ends." Is it really necessary that all rational beings must respect each other, and be bound by the same moral law? Kant's theory implies that if there are other rational beings elsewhere in the universe, they must recognize the categorical imperative if they reflect sufficiently, because it is built into their a priori reason, just as it is (allegedly) built into ours. It seems unlikely to me that all reflective rational beings would endorse the categorical imperative. It seems perfectly possible that reflective rational beings, elsewhere in the universe, might discover us on our insignificant planet and decide to treat us roughly as we treat shrimp. That is, they might find us tasty and abundant and decide to harvest us and eat us (with cocktail sauce). Kant apparently thinks that even if they did this, these other rational beings would have to feel guilty, because, deep in their a priori reason, they would know it was wrong. I don't buy it. Science fiction here seems deeper and more disturbing than anything in Kant's philosophy.

Another problem: "ought" implies "can," and doesn't Kant believe that events in the empirical world are causally determined? How, then, can a rational being choose whether to conform his actions to the categorical imperative or not? Determinism would seem to imply that some people will be moral and some people won't, but it isn't really up to us. How can you have autonomy in a deterministic world?

Recall that, according to Kant, the self has a noumenal aspect that is outside causality. Despite the fact that the will is determined in its actions as an empirical phenomenon, Kant thinks it makes sense to hold people morally responsible for their bad deeds and to punish them retributively, because this noumenal soul exists and is somehow ultimately responsible. Kant also notes that even though freedom (in the sense of open futures) cannot be proven, we must presuppose such freedom for practical purposes; deliberation isn't really possible without freedom as a practical posit.[23] Accordingly, the world of morality and responsibility is a peculiarly incoherent one. We must simultaneously, and inconsistently, consider ourselves from two different perspectives. This strikes some people as profound, but it strikes me as deeply unsatisfactory.

The following is popularly (though confusedly) taken to be a lasting legacy of Kant's moral philosophy: respecting the autonomy of rational beings is important. Achieving the greatest happiness for the greatest number, the end of all moral action according to consequentialists, is not the only thing to be taken into account in deciding what to do. If achieving the greatest happiness for the greatest number would involve violating the rights of some rational being, then so much the worse for the greatest happiness principle. Rational beings have rights, primarily the right to be let alone to pursue their own good in their own way, as long as they aren't harming anybody else in the process.[24]

I certainly believe this is correct, but my question is: What does *this* notion of autonomy (so central to liberalism) have to do with *Kant's* notion of autonomy? For Kant, autonomy means the (fictional) ability to conform one's conduct to some (fictional) absolute law, a law making reference to no inclination and to no end. This makes no sense and has nothing to do with liberty rights, which is what "autonomy" means to most people, and the sense in which it is an important moral concept.

Schopenhauer Reads Kant's Ethics

Recall that the clearest statement of Schopenhauer's ethical views, along with his critique of Kantian ethics, appears in the essay he wrote for a contest sponsored by the Royal Danish Society of Scientific Studies. Schopenhauer begins his critique of Kantian ethics on a generous note, by specifying what he takes to be the two

---

23. Kant, *Foundations*, pp. 66–67.

24. For a ringing defense of this notion of autonomy, written by a eudaimonistic utilitarian, see John Stuart Mill, *On Liberty* (Indianapolis: Hackett, 1978).

chief merits of Kant's moral philosophy. First, says Schopenhauer, Kant at least tried to purge ethics of eudaimonism (the view that moral action aims at happiness, understood as activity of soul in accordance with uniquely human excellences). Second, Kant noticed that human moral conduct has a deep significance that somehow touches on the thing-in-itself.[25]

Why, exactly, does Schopenhauer think so little of eudaimonism? Why does he think Kant was on the right track in trying to get rid of it? According to Schopenhauer, all the ancients except Plato tried to prove that virtue was a means to happiness, and Schopenhauer thinks this can't be done, since virtue is not a means to happiness. Why not? This is not clear at the present point. I suggest we put off a discussion of Schopenhauer's notions of virtue and happiness until we finish with his critique of Kant; only then will we be prepared to discuss his positive moral doctrine.

Plato's ethics, Schopenhauer states, was not eudaimonistic, but rather mystical, and was therefore superior. Recall that Plato teaches that the Form of the Good is the highest of all Forms, the reality that illuminates all other realities and makes them intelligible, as the sun illuminates the material world and makes it visible.[26] This is a very difficult doctrine to understand, but it has the implication that there is really no problem about fitting value into a world of facts, because value is built into the facts. Metaphysics and morals are (somehow) *one*. Schopenhauer is deeply sympathetic to this (difficult to express) idea.

Schopenhauer notes that, with regard to Kant, he finds *Foundations of the Metaphysics of Morals* more intelligible than the *Critique of Practical Reason*, expressing the opinion that by the time Kant wrote the latter work, his mental powers were deteriorating due to old age. He proposes to examine the *Foundations* point by point, destroying Kant's arguments, before going on to present his own ideas regarding the metaphysical basis of morality.

Kant's first false step is to beg an important question by assuming that there are moral laws, laws specifying how things ought to be, even if things never are this way in actual fact. Schopenhauer reacts with empiricist incredulity: Who says there are such laws? Our only source of information is experience, and experience tells

25. Schopenhauer, *On the Basis of Morality*, trans. E. F. J. Payne (Indianapolis: Hackett, 1995), pp. 49–50.

26. See Plato's *Republic*, Books VI and VII.

us only how things are, not how things should be. The only law to which human beings are obviously subject, says Schopenhauer, is the law of causality (action ensues only in the presence of the appropriate motivation), and this is not a moral law, but simply a law of nature. Kant has made a crucial error in assuming that the goal of moral philosophy is to find laws prescribing human conduct, to seek something in legislative, imperative form. According to Schopenhauer, this is the subtle route by which Kant smuggles theological assumptions into his ethics. Prescriptive law requires a lawgiver. Kant is assuming a Judeo-Christian God, and the concept of morality as the commands of such a God, without ever making this assumption explicit. It is all built into the idea of morality as law, or imperative, or command.[27]

Schopenhauer finds it incredible that Kant could assert "thou shalt not lie" is a law, carrying with it absolute necessity. Necessity, says Schopenhauer, means "characterized by the inevitability of the resulting effect." But how can such a notion attach to moral rules, since everybody (even Kant) must admit that in actual practice everybody disobeys moral imperatives all the time? The whole notion of moral necessity is so obscure as to be meaningless.

Kant's assumption that there are absolute moral duties is another example of the same kind of question-begging Kant engages in with regard to the (closely related) notion of law. With regard to the concept of duty, Schopenhauer says: "This concept, together with its near relatives, such as those of law, command, obligation, and so on, taken in this unconditional sense, has its origin in theological morals, and remains a stranger to the philosophical until it has produced a valid credential from the essence of human nature or that of the objective world."[28]

According to Schopenhauer, every ought derives its force from some kind of incentive. The natural reaction to a command ("Thou shalt do such-and-such") is to ask, "*Why* should I do such-and-such? What will I, or someone else, get out of it? What will happen if I disobey?" Thus, it seems to Schopenhauer (just as it seems to me) that every ought is necessarily conditioned, and accordingly, every imperative is necessarily hypothetical: "Do this, *if* you want to achieve result x or avoid consequence y." The notion of a categorical imperative is a contradiction in terms.

27. Schopenhauer, *On the Basis of Morality*, pp. 52–54.
28. Schopenhauer, *On the Basis of Morality*, p. 54.

Schopenhauer thinks that Kant secretly recognizes this and is smuggling in the notion that God will punish wrongdoers, and reward the righteous, in immortality.[29] Without this hidden assumption, the whole system makes no sense:

> The complete, utter impossibility and absurdity of this concept of an *unconditioned obligation* that underlies Kant's ethics appears later in his system itself, in the *Critique of Practical Reason*, like a concealed poison that cannot remain in the organism, but must finally break out and show itself. Thus that *ought*, said to be so *unconditioned*, nevertheless in the background postulates a condition, and indeed more than one, namely, a reward, plus the immortality of the person to be rewarded, and a rewarder.[30]

In the *Critique of Practical Reason*, Kant argues that the existence of God and the immortality of the soul, while these are metaphysical doctrines that cannot be proven, are nonetheless necessary "postulates of practical reason": we must believe these things on faith, in order to have the necessary incentive to obey the moral law.[31] Here, Kant admits what he did not admit in *Foundations*: that we need an incentive to obey moral rules. This effectively undermines the whole notion of a categorical imperative.

Also in the *Critique of Practical Reason*, Kant introduces the notion of the "highest good." He suggests that the person who is virtuous (follows "the moral law," as Kant conceives of it) is also the happiest of human beings. Not only is the virtuous person uniquely worthy to be happy; he *is* happy.[32] According to Schopenhauer, this is another instance of Kant smuggling in an incentive to obey the (supposedly unconditioned) moral law: be moral, because that's the only way you'll every really be happy. Thus, Kant turns out to be a closet consequentialist. Whereas Kant purports to purge philosophy of eudaimonism, he does this "more in appearance than in reality."[33] Kant officially rejects eudaimonism at the beginning of his system; then he allows it to creep back in through the rear door, under the name of "the highest good."[34]

---

29. Schopenhauer, *On the Basis of Morality*, p. 55.

30. Schopenhauer, *On the Basis of Morality*, p. 55.

31. Kant, *Critique of Practical Reason*, trans. Lewis White Beck (Upper Saddle River, N.J.: Prentice-Hall, 1993), pp. 128, 130.

32. Kant, *Critique of Practical Reason*, p. 117.

33. Schopenhauer, *On the Basis of Morality*, p. 49.

34. Schopenhauer, *On the Basis of Morality*, p. 56.

Schopenhauer's characterization of Kant's method is memorably amusing:

> [F]rom theological morals Kant had borrowed [the] imperative form of ethics tacitly and without examining it. The hypotheses of such morals and hence theology really underlie that form, and in fact...they are inseparable from it....After this he then had at the end of his discussion an easy task of again developing from his morals a theology, the well-known moral theology. For then he needed only to bring out expressly the concepts that lay hidden at the base of his morals, implicitly put there by the *ought* or *obligation*, and state them explicitly as postulates of practical reason. And so there appeared, to the great edification of the world, a theology resting merely on morals, in fact derived from it. But this came about because this morality itself rested on concealed theological hypotheses.... [T]he case is analogous to the surprise prepared for us by a conjurer, when he allows us to find a thing in a place in which he, in his capacity as conjurer, had previously put it.[35]

According to Schopenhauer, this conjuring trick[36] was so confusing that nobody, not even Kant himself, quite recognized the deception. In all Kant's turgid prose, no great reasoning has been performed. At the end, the familiar Judeo-Christian moral code of the Ten Commandments and the Golden Rule pops out, but this is indeed a magic trick. All of Kant's tortured reasoning has failed to give it a grounding in a priori reason.

Schopenhauer compares Kant to a doctor who once achieves success with a particular treatment and thereafter applies this same treatment to every disease. The separation of a priori from a posteriori knowledge was so useful in epistemology that Kant tried to make it work for ethics, too. But in ethics it is wholly inappropriate. How could pure reason (which provides only the form of knowledge, not the content) possibly contain a rule of conduct, such as the categorical imperative? How could ethics gain any content at all, except from empirical study of humankind and the world?

> [Kant] establishes his moral principle—and to this I wish to draw attention—not on any demonstrable *fact of consciousness*, such as an inner disposition, or yet on any objective relation of things in the

---

35. Schopenhauer, *On the Basis of Morality*, p. 57.

36. One may be reminded here of Wittgenstein's parenthetical remark in *Philosophical Investigations* 308: "The decisive move in the conjuring-trick has been made, and it was the very one that we thought quite innocent."

external world. No! This would be an empirical foundation. On the contrary, *pure concepts a priori*, in other words, concepts containing nothing at all from outer or inner experience and so mere shells without kernels, are to be the basis of morals.... [W]hat are we to hold onto? Onto a few concepts which are entirely abstract, wholly insubstantial, and likewise floating entirely in air. It is from these, indeed really from the mere form of their connection with judgments, that a *law* is said to result. It is supposed to be valid with so-called *absolute necessity*, and to have the power to put bridle and bit on the impulse of strong desires, the storm of passion, and the gigantic stature of egoism. We will certainly look into this.[37]

Schopenhauer points out that the a priori forms of space, time, and causality may indeed be seen as necessary, since we cannot imagine any experience without them. Relegating an ethical law to the sphere of the synthetic a priori, however, is an entirely different matter, since plenty of people seem blissfully unaware of this alleged moral law and disobey it with impunity. What can necessity mean in such a context?[38] Furthermore, even if the form of a rule were hard-wired in rational beings, that rule would be empty of content without some input from experience, and it is incomprehensible how the empty form of a rule could motivate human conduct.[39]

Schopenhauer also expresses skepticism regarding Kant's idea that this alleged a priori moral law would be binding on all rational beings, whoever they might be ("the dear little angels"?). If it originates in human cognitive faculties, why think it applies outside the human species?[40]

Kant's assertion that an action only has moral worth if performed from an austere sense of duty, rather than from any tenderheartedness or inclination, is as incomprehensible to Schopenhauer as it is to me. Schopenhauer also notes that if Kant were right about the synthetic a priori nature of the categorical imperative, then this alleged moral law would concern only the phenomenal world and would have absolutely nothing to do with the thing-in-itself. Yet, Kant insists on a thesis, inconsistent with this, with which Schopenhauer agrees: human moral conduct somehow touches on noumenal reality.[41]

37. Schopenhauer, *On the Basis of Morality*, p. 62.
38. Schopenhauer, *On the Basis of Morality*, p. 53.
39. Schopenhauer, *On the Basis of Morality*, pp. 75–76.
40. Schopenhauer, *On the Basis of Morality*, p. 63.
41. Schopenhauer, *On the Basis of Morality*, pp. 65–66.

Schopenhauer also complains that Kant rests the postulate of human freedom on the existence of the moral law ("you ought, therefore you can"), but there is absolutely no independent reason to believe in either freedom of the will, or in any absolute a priori moral law. Kant's concepts of moral law and freedom must sink together, since they are twin fictions, supported by nothing but each other.

The Kantian idea that rationality is identical with virtue strikes Schopenhauer as ludicrous:

> [T]he term *reasonable* or *rational* has at all times been applied to that man who does not allow himself to be guided by the impressions of *intuitive perception*, but by *thoughts* and *concepts*, and who therefore always goes to work thoughtfully, consistently, and deliberately....But this by no means implies uprightness and love for one's fellows. On the contrary, a man can go to work very rationally...and yet act upon the most selfish, unjust, and even iniquitous maxims....Reasonable and vicious are quite consistent with each other; in fact, only through their union are great and far-reaching crimes possible.[42]

Like me, Schopenhauer fails to see the "contradictions" supposedly involved in Kant's examples of violations of alleged "absolute duties." Insofar as there is anything repugnant about, say, failing to be charitable to others in need, it is not a rational contradiction but an affront to egoism, since I would want others to help me if I were in need. If the basis of moral rules thus turns out to be disguised egoism (as Hobbes thought), this is certainly not what Kant had in mind, yet Kant's examples fail to support any other conclusion. The "categorical" imperative turns out to be, in the end, hypothetical: if you want others to be truthful with you, tell the truth; if you want others to be kind to you, be kind to others; if you want others not to cheat you, don't cheat them. However, there is absolutely no contradiction involved in ignoring these counsels, if one has the power to get away with it: "[I]f I do away with this condition...confident perhaps of my superior mental and bodily strength...I can very well will injustice and uncharitableness as a universal maxim, and accordingly rule the world."[43]

The above constitutes Schopenhauer's main criticism of Kantian ethics. Much of *On the Basis of Morality* consists of repetition of these

---

42. Schopenhauer, *On the Basis of Morality*, p. 83.
43. Schopenhauer, *On the Basis of Morality*, p. 91.

arguments in different words, with increasing exasperation and sarcastic rhetorical flourishes. (One can almost see Schopenhauer tearing at the tufts of white hair growing out of each side of his head.)

Compassion as the Basis of Ethics

Despite his obvious sympathy for the mystical notion that metaphysics and ethics are somehow one, Schopenhauer declares that a philosopher doing moral theory ought clearly to separate the *what* of ethics (the basic principles or rules of conduct) from the *why* (the metaphysical grounding, the reason behind the rules).[44] He opines that everybody really agrees about the *what*—it is something like this: hurt no one, and help everyone as much as you can. This simple sentence is as far as Schopenhauer goes in trying to formulate the normative part of a moral theory. It is the *why*, the metaphysical part, that is problematic, and Schopenhauer hopes to give an illuminating answer to it.

Schopenhauer says that "there is no other way for discovering the foundation of ethics than the empirical, namely, to investigate whether there are generally any actions to which we must attribute *genuine moral worth*. Such will be actions of voluntary justice, pure philanthropy, and real magnanimity."[45]

Rejecting psychological egoism, Schopenhauer finds it most reasonable to interpret the evidence straightforwardly and to admit that there *are* genuinely moral actions, though not many.[46] In keeping with his realistic (or pessimistic) estimation of human beings generally, Schopenhauer notes that the vast majority of human actions are motivated by egoism, greed, vanity, and so forth. If it were not for the restraining influence of the law, most people would act very badly indeed, and it is with good reason that we fear anarchy. However, even in the worst of circumstances (e.g., anarchy), a few good people will continue to perform a few genuinely moral actions.[47]

44. Schopenhauer, *On the Basis of Morality*, pp. 68–69.
45. Schopenhauer, *On the Basis of Morality*, p. 130.
46. Schopenhauer, *On the Basis of Morality*, p. 126; see also pp. 138–139.
47. See Schopenhauer, *On the Basis of Morality*, pp. 121–130. On p. 126, Schopenhauer writes, "[T]here are really honest people just as there are actually four-leaved clover; but Hamlet does not exaggerate when he says, 'To be honest, as this world goes, is to be one man picked out of ten thousand.'"

Among antimoral incentives, egoism is chief. Schopenhauer agrees with Spinoza that the essence of a thing is its drive to keep itself in existence; this shows in humankind as what Freud would later call "id"—a psychological core that wants to enjoy everything, to have everything, to control everything.[48] Other antimoral incentives include ill will, envy, spitefulness, malicious joy at another's misfortune, and cruelty.[49] Opposing these powerful forces, so deeply seated in human nature, are two motives: fear of punishment or consequence, and genuine moral incentive. Given the strength and pervasiveness of the antimoral forces, it is rather remarkable that genuine moral incentive ever triumphs at all.[50]

For Schopenhauer, the defining criterion of an action with genuine moral worth is that it lacks self-interested motivation. He believes that (putting aside the caviling of the psychological egoist) such actions do occur, and we have experience of them. These are actions of "voluntary justice and disinterested loving-kindness," capable of rising to "nobleness and magnanimity."[51] The question we have to answer, he says, is what can possibly move a human being to action of this sort.[52]

Nowadays, sociobiologists attempt to account for the evolution of moral intuitions of justice and benevolence by theorizing that such psychological tendencies, appearing in the population due to random genetic mutations, proved conducive to strong social groups, thereby enabling individuals within those groups to survive and pass on their genes.[53] Schopenhauer offers a more metaphysical explanation. He says that for the welfare or distress of *another* to move *me*, I must recognize (in an emotional, mystical way antithetical to reason) that the other is the same as myself; we are both manifestations of the same underlying reality. This is the sense in which ethical conduct touches on the thing-in-itself. It breaks through the principle of individuation imposed on the world by cognition, and penetrates to the metaphysical secret that we all belong to the same Great Will.[54] Since nothing can be justified outside the structures imposed

---

48. Schopenhauer, *On the Basis of Morality*, p. 132.
49. Schopenhauer, *On the Basis of Morality*, pp. 134–135.
50. Schopenhauer, *On the Basis of Morality*, p. 137.
51. Schopenhauer, *On the Basis of Morality*, pp. 144–145.
52. Schopenhauer, *On the Basis of Morality*, p. 140.
53. See Kahane, "Sociobiology, Egoism, and Reciprocity," pp. 89–90.
54. Schopenhauer, *On the Basis of Morality*, pp. 203–214.

by reason, this mystical ethical insight, and the way people attain it, must remain, ultimately, a mystery. It is felt, not reasoned.[55] Schopenhauer argues that one of the merits of his proposal is that it includes nonhuman animals as proper objects of moral sentiment.[56] Indeed, Schopenhauer's ethics implies that all creation, living and nonliving, is included in the moral sphere.

I mentioned above that Schopenhauer is less than clear, in *On the Basis of Morality*, regarding his reasons for rejecting eudaimonism. Looking at Schopenhauer's other works, we can see that he identifies happiness with satisfaction of the ego, and virtue with the extinguishing of the ego. Accordingly, virtue can never be a means to happiness. Happiness is affirmation of the individual will, whereas true virtue is denial of the individual will. Schopenhauer also evidently believes that advocates of eudaimonistic ethics, such as Socrates and Aristotle, failed adequately to answer the egoist's challenge (to the effect that the nonmoral person who gets away with his injustice and does not care about anyone but himself is actually happier than the moral man).

Evaluative Remarks

Certainly, not all that Schopenhauer says in *On the Basis of Morality* is plausible or satisfying. One understands why the judges for the Royal Danish Society of Scientific Studies declined to award the essay a prize, despite the fact that it was the sole entry in the contest. In particular, there is a long discussion of the virtue of justice, attempting not very successfully to argue that justice is based in compassion, and containing some of Schopenhauer's unfortunate misogyny (he approvingly cites the common prejudice to the effect that women are less capable of justice and principled reasoning than men, and in general possess a weaker reasoning faculty than men).[57] He even remarks, "The very thought of seeing women administer justice raises a laugh."[58] I wish he could be magically transported to our time and observe some of our many fine women jurists. He also indulges in his habitual abuse of Fichte, Schelling, and Hegel,

55. Schopenhauer, *On the Basis of Morality*, p. 212.
56. Schopenhauer, *On the Basis of Morality*, p. 175.
57. Schopenhauer, *On the Basis of Morality*, pp. 148–162.
58. Schopenhauer, *On the Basis of Morality*, p. 151.

which, while we may find it amusing, is definitely not polite. He calls Fichte and Schelling "dishonest" men whose method consists in "mystifying, producing an impression, misleading, throwing dust in the eyes, and bragging." He calls Hegel a "clumsy and senseless charlatan."[59] No wonder the Royal Danish Society, in its judgment, noted, "We cannot pass over in silence the fact that several distinguished philosophers of recent times are mentioned in a manner so unseemly as to cause just and grave offense."[60]

However, did Schopenhauer really fail to answer the question asked by the society, as charged in the judgment? The question posed was, "Are the source and foundation of morals to be looked for in an idea of morality lying immediately in consciousness (or conscience) and in the analysis of the other fundamental moral concepts springing from that idea, or are they to be looked for in a different ground of knowledge?" Given the confusing nature of the question, it is no wonder Schopenhauer was the only entrant, and I must say, I think he answered the question pretty well on the whole (though he would have benefited from an editor). His criticisms of Kantian ethics are the best and most penetrating I have ever seen. His conclusion that compassion is at the heart of morality is in agreement with modern social science, which tells us that sociopaths (a.k.a. evil people) are defective precisely in lacking empathy.

What may strike some readers as least satisfying about Schopenhauer's ethics is the appeal to extrarational mystical insight. Schopenhauer's metaphysics of Will shares this same flaw (if it is a flaw). Ultimately, there is no argument for something you just *feel*, and there's no way you can convince someone who doesn't already feel it, too. Thus, the Royal Danish Society accused Schopenhauer of failing to show that his foundation for morality was adequate.

But is *any* foundation for morality wholly adequate? Even the moral theory I find most appealing on the whole, the deontological intuitionism of W. D. Ross, fails to explain *why* reflective nonsociopaths have the basic moral intuitions we do. These intuitions are just given, they are the data of moral theory—this is what we really think and feel.

It may seem dangerous to rest moral theory on mere intuition, but what is the alternative? Unless we can find a set of basic moral

59. Schopenhauer, *On the Basis of Morality*, p. 80.
60. The judgment is included at the end of the 1995 Hackett edition of *On the Basis of Morality*. The passage quoted is on p. 216.

intuitions, widely shared among reflective people, what *data* will there be to constrain moral theory? We must appeal to reflective intuition in evaluating moral theories, just as we appeal to empirical observation in evaluating scientific theories. Schopenhauer points out that a mystical sense of oneness with all creation is a widely shared moral intuition. This is not itself a moral theory, but it is an important part of the grounding of any adequate moral theory—if such a thing as an "adequate moral theory" is possible, which Schopenhauer surely doubted.

Wittgenstein's Ethical View and Its Schopenhauerian Roots

In his *Tractatus*, Wittgenstein makes some intriguing and enigmatic remarks about ethics, the meaning of life, and the mystical. These occur at 6.4 and following. Some examples: "It is impossible to speak about the will insofar as it is the subject of ethical attributes" (6.423). "When the answer cannot be put into words, neither can the question be put into words. *The riddle* does not exist. If a question can be framed at all, it is also *possible* to answer it" (6.5). "We feel that even when all *possible* scientific questions have been answered, the problems of life remain completely untouched. Of course there are then no questions left, and this itself is the answer" (6.52). "There are, indeed, things that cannot be put into words. They make themselves manifest. They are what is mystical" (6.522).[61]

In 1929, eight years after the *Tractatus* was first published, Wittgenstein gave a lecture on ethics to the Heretics Society in Cambridge.[62] This lecture, taken together with the remarks in the *Tractatus*, reveals that Wittgenstein denies moral *theory* to be possible. He believes ethics concerns matters that cannot be expressed in language. Wittgenstein's views here have a strongly Schopenhauerian flavor. It is hard to avoid the suspicion that much of what Wittgenstein says about ethics, as well as about "saying" and

61. Ludwig Wittgenstein, *Tractatus Logico-Philosophicus*, trans. D. F. Pears and B. F. McGuinness (London: Routledge, 1961), pp. 72–73.

62. See Wittgenstein, "Lecture on Ethics," in *Ludwig Wittgenstein: Philosophical Occasions 1912–1951*, ed. James Klagge and Alfred Nordmann (Indianapolis: Hackett, 1993), pp. 37–44. Wittgenstein wrote his notes for this lecture in English, not his native tongue. The text contains some grammatical infelicities that Klagge and Nordmann have preserved.

"showing," is subliminally derived from his reading of Schopenhauer as a young man.

Let us look at Wittgenstein's lecture on ethics. He begins by contrasting what he calls "relative judgments of value" with "absolute judgments of value." The former, a relative judgment of value, is something like, "This is a good chair," meaning, this item of furniture serves its purpose (to be sat upon). According to Wittgenstein, such relative claims of value simply *state facts*. To say, "This is a good chair," is just another way of saying that I can sit on it, it won't break, it is reasonably comfortable, and so on. There is nothing metaphysically mysterious about such relative judgments of value. They reduce to statements of fact.

The latter, an absolute judgment of value, is illustrated by Wittgenstein with the following story: "[S]uppose I had told one of you a preposterous lie and he came up to me and said, 'You're behaving like a beast,' and then I were to say, 'I know I behave badly, but then I don't want to behave any better,' could he then say, 'Ah, then that's all right'? Certainly not; he would say, 'Well, you *ought* to want to behave better.' Here you have an absolute judgment of value."[63] Wittgenstein goes on to maintain that although all judgments of relative value can be reduced to statements of fact, no statement of fact can ever be, or imply, a judgment of absolute value. A complete description of the world, he argues, would contain nothing we could call an absolute judgment of value (a truly *ethical* judgment), or anything that would imply such a judgment. It would contain only relative judgments of value, which can be explained away as disguised statements of fact.

Is Wittgenstein merely agreeing with Hamlet that "nothing is either good or bad but thinking makes it so"? Wittgenstein says no; his point is deeper: "What Hamlet says seems to imply that good and bad, though not qualities of the world outside us, are attributes to [sic] our states of mind. But what I mean is that a state of mind, so far as we mean by that a fact which we can describe, is in no ethical sense good or bad."[64]

Suppose the complete description of the world contains an account of a vicious murder, including all the facts, physical and psychological. Wittgenstein says that the mere description of these facts will contain nothing that is, properly speaking, an *ethical* proposition.

63. Wittgenstein, "Lecture on Ethics," p. 39.
64. Wittgenstein, "Lecture on Ethics," p. 39.

The murder, whatever emotions provoked it, and whatever emotions it provokes in us, is simply a fact, on the same level as the falling of a stone:

> There will simply be facts, facts, facts, but no Ethics.... [I]f I contemplate what Ethics really would have to be if there were such a science, this result seems to me quite obvious.... [N]othing we could ever think or say should be *the* thing.... I can only describe my feeling by the metaphor, that, if a man could write a book on Ethics which really was a book on Ethics, this book would, with an explosion, destroy all the other books in the world.[65]

Wittgenstein argues that if there were such a thing in the world as an *absolute good*, and if this thing were a describable state of affairs, then everybody, regardless of his personal tastes and inclinations, would feel compelled to try to bring it about and feel guilty if they failed to do so. But no *fact* has such coercive normative power, and the world consists only of facts.[66]

Nevertheless, people feel tempted to use such expressions as "absolute good," and Wittgenstein counts himself among such people. He tries to articulate what he, personally, means by such an expression. He says there is one kind of *experience* that, for him, seems to have absolute value. This is an experience of wondering at the existence of the world. Wittgenstein also mentions a feeling of being absolutely safe, of feeling, "Nothing can injure me whatever happens."[67]

Strictly speaking, says Wittgenstein, it is nonsense to say things like, "I am amazed at the existence of the world," or "I feel that I am absolutely safe, and nothing can injure me": "[I]t is nonsense to say that I wonder at the existence of the world, because I cannot imagine it not existing.... To be safe essentially means that it is physically impossible that certain things should happen to me and therefore it's nonsense to say that I am safe *whatever* happens."[68]

---

65. Wittgenstein, "Lecture on Ethics," p. 40.

66. The reader may be reminded here of J. L. Mackie's "argument from queerness." See Mackie, *Ethics: Inventing Right and Wrong* (New York: Penguin Books, 1976).

67. Wittgenstein's mention of the feeling of being *absolutely safe* reminds me of an obscure remark Schopenhauer makes: "[I]t is just as impossible for us to fall out of existence as it is for us to fall out of space." This sounds like something Wittgenstein himself might have said! See Schopenhauer, *WWR*, vol. 2, p. 489.

68. Wittgenstein, "Lecture on Ethics," pp. 41–42.

According to Wittgenstein, "[a] certain characteristic misuse of our language runs through all ethical and religious expressions."[69] Ethical and religious expressions can often be construed as similes; for example, to say that I feel safe in the hands of God is just to say that I feel *as if* I were in the hands of a loving, omnipotent being. However, in the case of what Wittgenstein is calling a truly ethical claim, an absolute judgment of value, there exists no fact to give meaning to the simile: "[A] simile must be the simile *for* something. And if I can describe a fact by means of a simile I must also be able to drop the simile and to describe the facts without it. Now in our case as soon as we try to drop the simile and simply to state the facts which stand behind it, we find that there are no such facts. And so, what appeared to be a simile now seems to be mere nonsense."[70]

Experiences, says Wittgenstein, are facts. Many people would agree that there are experiences of the kind Wittgenstein mentions (experiences of wondering at the existence of the world, or feeling absolutely safe), and most of these people would want to say that such experiences possess absolute value. "It is the [*sic*] paradox that an experience, a fact, should seem to have supernatural value."[71]

Wittgenstein suggests an alternative way of characterizing the experience of wondering at the existence of the world: experiencing the world as a miracle. When we look at the world in a scientific way, as an array of facts to be described, everything miraculous disappears. The scientific way of looking at the world is not the right way to look, if we want to see miracles. In this context, Wittgenstein says something mysterious:

> Now I am tempted to say that the right expression in language for the miracle of the existence of the world, though it is not any proposition *in* language, is the existence of language itself.... [A]ll I have said by shifting the expression of the miraculous from an expression *by means of* language to the expression [of] *the existence* of language [is] that we cannot express what we want to express and that all we *say* about the absolute miraculous [*sic*] remains nonsense.[72]

Wittgenstein concludes the lecture by saying that the nonsensicality of ethical expressions is their very essence, because such expressions seek to go beyond the world, beyond significant language.

69. Wittgenstein, "Lecture on Ethics," p. 42.
70. Wittgenstein, "Lecture on Ethics," p. 43.
71. Wittgenstein, "Lecture on Ethics," p. 43.
72. Wittgenstein, "Lecture on Ethics," pp. 43–44.

Anyone who tries to talk or write about religion or ethics (e.g., anyone who attempts theology or ethical theory) runs up against the boundaries of language. The key things *cannot be said.* So, ethics can never be a science, or anything resembling a science. "What [ethics] says cannot add to our knowledge in any sense. But it is a document of a tendency in the human mind which I personally cannot help respecting deeply and I would not for my life ridicule it."[73]

Let us return to the *Tractatus.* In that work, Wittgenstein utilizes the distinction between "saying" and "showing" in (at least) two different contexts. The first context is discussion of propositions expressed in either natural language or the formal languages of logic. Propositions in natural language (at least the nontautologous ones) *say* something, and also *show* something. "A proposition *shows* its sense. A proposition *shows* how things stand *if* it is true. And it *says* that they do so stand" (4.022). "Propositions cannot represent logical form: it is mirrored in them.... Propositions *show* the logical form of reality; they display it" (4.121).

Propositions of logic (truth-functionally true statements, or valid arguments expressed as their corresponding material conditionals) *say* nothing. "The propositions of logic are tautologies" (6.1). "[T]he propositions of logic say nothing. (They are the analytic propositions)" (6.11).

However, the propositions of logic, the tautologies, *show* something important: "The fact that the propositions of logic are tautologies *shows* the formal—logical—properties of language and the world" (6.12; see also 6.124). Here Wittgenstein implies that logic reveals not just the structure of the world, the totality of contingent facts, but the necessary structure of reality, of all possible worlds.

Elsewhere, Wittgenstein speaks in terms of *limits* of language and the world and sometimes uses the words "manifest" or "signify" instead of the similar "show." For example: "Empirical reality is limited by the totality of objects. The limit also makes itself manifest in the totality of elementary propositions" (5.5561). "*The limits of my language* mean the limits of my world. Logic pervades the world: the limits of the world are also its limits.... We cannot think what we cannot think; so what we cannot think we cannot *say* either" (5.6; 5.61). "Philosophy sets limits to the much disputed sphere of natural science" (4.113). "It must set limits to what can be thought;

and, in doing so, to what cannot be thought. It must set limits to what cannot be thought by working outwards through what can be thought" (4.114). "It will signify what cannot be said, by presenting clearly what can be said" (4.115).

Beginning at 6.4, Wittgenstein begins to discuss ethics. Here are some relevant remarks we have not already surveyed: "All propositions are of equal value" (6.4). "[I]t is impossible for there to be propositions of ethics. Propositions can express nothing higher" (6.42). "It is clear that ethics cannot be put into words. Ethics is transcendental. (Ethics and aesthetics are one and the same)" (6.421).

Can I justify my suspicion that all this derives originally from Schopenhauer? Recall two key theses of Schopenhauer: (1) ethics touches on the thing-in-itself, in the intuitive recognition that we are all part of the same great Will; and (2) the nature of the thing-in-itself (the world as Will) *shows* itself in the nature of the phenomenal world, the world as representation. Once again, I call the reader's attention to the clearest statement of this view, which occurs in the appendix (Criticism of the Kantian Philosophy) to volume 1 of *WWR* (p. 428 in the Payne translation). Schopenhauer explicitly uses the word "limit" here, as he often does, to characterize the self. Sometimes he says the self is the metaphysical limit of the world; here he seems to say that the self is a boundary condition placing unspecified constraints on knowledge.

At any rate, the main point of the passage is that one obtains metaphysical knowledge (knowledge of the thing-in-itself) by *looking* at that which is not the thing-in-itself. The source of metaphysical knowledge is observation of the world—the same as the source of empirical science. Thus, Schopenhauer clearly holds that we can gain knowledge about something "unspeakable" by comprehending the "speakable" and its limits.

There is another intriguing section of the appendix where Schopenhauer says, "Grammar is related to logic as clothes are to the body," and goes on to maintain that thoughts have a logical form beneath the superficial structures imposed by various natural languages:

> [G]rammar explains only the clothing of the forms of thought; hence the parts of speech can be derived from the original thought-forms themselves, which are independent of all languages; their function is to express these forms of thought with all their modifications....

...Philosophical grammar has to tell us about the precise mechanism of the expression of the thought-forms, just as logic has to inform us about the operations with the thought-forms themselves.[74]

Schopenhauer's point in this section seems to be that both natural language, and the "thought-forms" or deep structures underlying surface grammar, reveal to us the Kantian categories (which, for Schopenhauer, are located in the faculty of reason). Such categories limit what can be said, and hence they limit the sphere of propositional reasoning.

Of course, if one has read the rest of *WWR*, one knows that "the riddle of the world," the most important question of all, cannot really be put into words and hence cannot be the subject of propositional reasoning. The "riddle" begins with a kind of wonderment at our own existence and the existence of the world. Its subject matter is outside the Kantian categories.

Earlier in *WWR*, Schopenhauer remarks that when we look at the world as representation, we want to know its *significance*: Is the world nothing more than representation, or is there something beyond it?[75] This, of course, is the metaphysical question, one aspect of "the riddle." We can see that it is literally an unaskable question, since the objects and events making up the world as representation are the only things we can talk about, the only referents for concepts and words. Somehow, we can have a question in our minds that is literally nonsense, yet it is the most important question of all. And, according to Schopenhauer, the metaphysical question and the ethical question are really the same question, two aspects of "the riddle."

The general theme of trying to get at what is unsayable (the thing-in-itself; ethics; aesthetics) by apprehending the limits of the sayable runs all through Schopenhauer's work. This theme was taken over by Wittgenstein in the *Tractatus*. What seems odd, and unjust, is that so few people seem to realize Schopenhauer is the original source of the theme.

74. *WWR*, vol. 1, appendix, pp. 478–480.
75. *WWR*, vol. 1, bk. 2, p. 98.

CHAPTER FOUR

Schopenhauer's Aesthetics

The Meaning of Art and Music

Schopenhauer's Aesthetic Theory in General

Schopenhauer maintains that the fine arts in general, including architecture, sculpture, painting, poetry, and literature, aim to present the Platonic Forms (or Ideas), which Schopenhauer takes to be various degrees of the Will's objectification.[1]

We have already seen in chapter 1 that Schopenhauer's doctrine of the Platonic Forms is problematic. He tells us that these Forms show the Will "under the form of representation in general."[2] While independent of the Principle of Sufficient Reason, the Forms are still representations and therefore not quite noumenal; they are not exactly "out there" in the world wholly independent of the human mind, but rather are the most fundamental creations of cognition. This insistence is in tension with Schopenhauer's view that the forces of nature, including not only gravity and electromagnetism but chemical and biological kinds, are the noumenal reality, the original power lurking behind all causal explanations and presupposed by them; objective levels of what we know in ourselves as *will*.[3]

---

1. See generally *The World as Will and Representation* (hereafter *WWR*), vol. 1, bk. 3: "The World as Representation, Second Aspect: The Representation Independent of the Principle of Sufficient Reason: The Platonic Idea: The Object of Art."

2. *WWR*, vol. 1, p. 175.

3. See, e.g., *WWR*, vol. 1, p. 124, where Schopenhauer says, discussing the basic forces of nature: "[I]n everything in nature there is something to which no

Schopenhauer thinks art is important because it has metaphysical significance. The artist intuits the "one thought" at the heart of Schopenhauer's philosophical system, the sameness of the inner nature of all things. What the artist tries to communicate in his work is not only the "in-itself" of nature, but the artist's own self pared down to its essence. The artist does not learn through *experience* which forms in nature are beautiful, hence what to imitate in his work; rather, the artist has a priori knowledge of the beautiful, and this is a priori knowledge of a special kind—it concerns not the form of knowledge, but its content. This kind of knowledge is possible only because we ourselves are the Will. We feel that we ourselves are what nature attempts to present in all its forms. The artistic genius takes this feeling to its heights; he "understands nature's half-spoken words. He expresses clearly what she merely stammers. He impresses on the hard marble the beauty of the form which nature failed to achieve in a thousand attempts, and he places it before her, exclaiming as it were, 'This is what you desired to say!' And from the man who knows comes the echoing reply, 'Yes, that is it!' "[4]

This a priori understanding of beauty in the artist and its a posteriori recognition by the connoisseur depend on the fact that artist and connoisseur are themselves the Will objectifying itself. They are able to intuit what Schopenhauer calls the Platonic Forms or Ideas because they are themselves the highest levels of that objectification.[5] Art is, then, a sort of inarticulate metaphysics; it *shows* what the true philosophy *says*.[6]

---

ground can ever be assigned, for which no explanation is possible, and no further cause is to be sought. This something is the specific mode of the thing's action, in other words, the very manner of its existence, its being or true essence....But this, I say, is...what man's *will* is to a man; and, like the human will, it is in its inner nature not subject to explanation; indeed, it is in itself identical with this will." This sounds pretty noumenal to me, especially in view of Schopenhauer's central teaching that the thing-in-itself is will. This kind of equivocation about the nature of the Platonic Forms runs throughout the second book of *WWR* and has its genesis in *On the Fourfold Root of the Principle of Sufficient Reason*. See pp. 67–68 of the latter work, where Schopenhauer speaks of the basic forces of nature as noumenal, outside time, and "giving to causes their causality."

4. *WWR*, vol. 1, p. 222.
5. *WWR*, vol. 1, p. 222.
6. Here again, it is pretty obvious that Schopenhauer's work is the origin of the saying/showing distinction made so much of by Wittgenstein. See particularly *WWR*, vol. 2, pp. 406–407.

The Will objectifies itself at the lowest level, says Schopenhauer, as basic physical forces: gravity, cohesion, rigidity, hardness, light, fluidity. Architecture and landscape design, considered as fine arts (including the use of water in pools, streams, falls, etc.) aim to exhibit these fundamental Forms or Ideas.[7] Think of Frank Lloyd Wright's house Fallingwater, and perhaps it will seem to you (as it does to me) that Schopenhauer is onto something true: the best architecture dismisses with mere decoration and frippery and shows us weight and solidity, light and shadow, space and the filling up of space, the flow and reflective gleam of water—all basic properties of elemental matter. When we experience such architecture, we feel the same satisfaction that comes from contemplation of rock, sky, stream, and ocean in nature.

At the next level up, the Will objectifies itself as plants and non-human animals. These Ideas are exhibited, in plastic and visual art, by landscape painting and animal painting, and by sculpture of plant and animal forms.[8] Again, the pleasure we experience from these arts parallels the pleasure experienced in nature itself. Just as being in a park or wilderness, among trees and wild birds and animals, refreshes and delights us, so does seeing artistic representations of these living things. In general, Schopenhauer holds that aesthetic pleasure involves a "quieting" of the individual will—one's personal desires, struggles, and dissatisfactions fade into the background.

At the highest level, the Will objectifies itself as humanity and as the individual characters of particular human beings. Here Schopenhauer mentions historical painting, along with the painting and sculpture of human beauty, as the plastic arts that reveal these Forms to the intellect.[9]

Schopenhauer makes an intriguing distinction between the *beautiful* and the *sublime* (terms probably derived from Kant's Third Critique). An object is beautiful insofar as we can see, in it, the eternal Form and thus get beyond the individual. Appreciating beauty, we achieve "pure, will-less contemplation" devoid of individual interest. An object is sublime when it is beautiful but also hostile to the human will in general, that is, dangerous, threatening to overwhelm and destroy the individual, and yet the individual overcomes his fear for a while and can just *look* at the threatening

7. *WWR*, vol. 1, pp. 210, 214–217; see also vol. 2, pp. 411–418.
8. *WWR*, vol. 1, pp. 218–220.
9. *WWR*, vol. 1, pp. 220–221.

object or scene.[10] Examples of the sublime might be a predatory wild animal such as a tiger or grizzly bear (it could make a meal of us), a powerful storm (it could kill us), a hostile landscape such as a desert or arctic scene (we could not survive there), a view from a very high place (to fall would be deadly), or contemplation of the starry, airless infinity of space. Our perpetual, instinctive struggle against what is hostile to our life is (momentarily) swallowed up and not heeded; it goes unconscious. Instead of giving rise to fear, as it would normally, it gives rise to a quite different and more exalted feeling, the feeling of the sublime, involving a sense of oneness with the awful forces involved, and a temporary cessation of the fear of death.[11] (Here we see the relationship of Schopenhauer's concept of the sublime to the Freudian concept of sublimation—some powerful force or disturbance goes below the conscious level and serves ends other than normal.)

Schopenhauer holds that in aesthetic experience of either art or nature, we unconsciously recognize our kinship with the basic forces of nature and become no longer individual—in some obscure way, we merge with the great Will from which we sprang.[12] So much seems intuitively correct. What may seem incorrect (it seemed incorrect to me, for a long time) is Schopenhauer's notion that in such contemplation the viewer manages to detach himself from the Will entirely, to become "the clear mirror of the object."[13] According to Schopenhauer, it is this detachment from all willing that explains the peace of mind provided by art—again, art serves as a "quieter of all willing."[14] It seems incomprehensible how a creature whose very essence is willing could cease to will altogether. Elsewhere, Schopenhauer insists that cognition is a secondary adaptation of the will and always serves the will.[15] How, then, is the "pure, will-less

10. *WWR*, vol. 1, pp. 201–202.
11. *WWR*, vol. 1, pp. 205–206.
12. *WWR*, vol. 1, pp. 169, 176, 181.
13. *WWR*, vol. 1, p. 178.
14. *WWR*, vol. 1, p. 233; see also pp. 195–196.
15. *WWR*, vol. 1, p. 177: "[A]s a rule, knowledge remains subordinate to the service of the will, as indeed it came into being for this service; in fact, it sprang from the will, so to speak, as the head from the trunk." See also vol. 2, p. 205: "[I]n all animal beings the *will* is the primary and substantial thing; the *intellect*...is something secondary and additional, in fact a mere tool in the service of the will." As noted in chapter 1, this notion that intellect serves the (often unconscious) will is one of the Schopenhauerian doctrines most impressive to Freud.

contemplation" supposedly achieved in artistic appreciation possible? As rationally incomprehensible as it may be, it seems to be part of Schopenhauer's "single thought" that even though we *are* the Will, a kind of deliverance from willing is possible. It occurs momentarily in aesthetic experience and permanently in the saint or mystic who has reached "salvation."

Recently, I got up in the middle of the night and went outside to watch a total eclipse of the moon. Nobody else in the neighborhood had bothered to get up to watch the eclipse (maybe they didn't know about it). I was alone with the moon in the stillness of the night. During the eclipse, I think I got a fair idea of what Schopenhauer means when he describes an experience of the beautiful, or even of the sublime. All my personal worries and woes went away for a little while, as I watched the moon slowly drift into the shadow of the earth. A bright, full moon slowly became the thinnest of crescents, then disappeared, and there was a dusky, reddish disk, only faintly glowing...and then, it passed behind drifting clouds and was gone. I don't know why, but everything that torments me in my daily life—health and money problems for myself and my loved ones, for example—seemed suddenly nothing to worry about. The slow dance of the earth around the sun, and the moon around the earth, made the troubles of human beings seem like nothing more than a momentary, meaningless tickle in the great, indifferent universe. The stately motions of the heavenly bodies were going on long before I ever came to be, and would continue when I, and all people, were long gone. The eclipse didn't care if I was watching it or not. These thoughts did not make me sad; instead, they comforted me and made me feel completely unthreatened, absolutely safe.[16] Why? Why does an intuition of one's own insignificance bring divine peace?

Schopenhauer says that when we experience the sublime, not only do our individual troubles vanish, but we have the sudden intuition of ourselves as the limits and supporters of the world itself: "*The vastness of the world, which previously disturbed our peace of mind, now rests within us; our dependence on it is now annulled by its dependence on us.*"[17] I must say, I did not feel anything like that as I watched the eclipse of

---

16. Recall Wittgenstein's "Lecture on Ethics," discussed in chapter 3. "Feeling absolutely safe" is the phrase Wittgenstein uses to characterize one of the experiences he says has ethical value and can't adequately be put into words. My experience during the eclipse made me understand this for the first time.

17. *WWR*, vol. 1, p. 205.

the moon. Quite the contrary—rather than feeling I was myself the condition of the whole world's existence, the subject in whom the objects inhere, I felt that I was myself a very small part of a cosmos that depended on me in no way whatsoever. I think my feelings of insignificance, during experiences of the sublime, are rather more typical than Schopenhauer's feelings of grandiose importance.

The apparent contrast between my own realism and the Kantian anti-realism shared by Schopenhauer and the early Wittgenstein is surfacing at this point. Just as Schopenhauer conceives of the self as the metaphysical limit of the world, Wittgenstein says such things as "The world is *my* world" (5.62); "There is no such *thing* as the subject that thinks or entertains ideas" (5.631); "The subject does not belong to the world: rather, it is a limit of the world" (5.632); "The philosophical self is...the metaphysical subject, the limit of the world—not a part of it" (5.641).[18]

At 5.61 and 5.62, Wittgenstein says:

> We cannot think what we cannot think; so what we cannot think we cannot *say* either.... This remark provides the key to the problem, how much truth there is in solipsism. For what the solipsist *means* is quite correct; only it cannot be *said*, but makes itself manifest. The world is *my* world: this is manifest in the fact that the limits of *language* (of that language which alone I understand) mean the limits of *my* world.[19]

Wittgenstein goes on to say, at 5.64, "Here it can be seen that solipsism, when its implications are followed out strictly, coincides with pure realism. The self of solipsism shrinks to a point without extension, and there remains the reality coordinated with it."[20] What does Wittgenstein mean in this latter passage? Imagine a solipsist, A, exhaustively describing the world, and a "realist," B, doing the same. Their descriptions would be indistinguishable. It's just that each would *say* something different at the end:

A: "Oh, by the way, it's all in the mind."
B: "Oh, by the way, it's all outside the mind."

So, maybe the contrast between my own realism and the anti-realism shared by Schopenhauer and Wittgenstein is more apparent than

18. Ludwig Wittgenstein, *Tractatus Logico-Philosophicus*, trans. D. F. Pears and B. F. McGuinness (London: Routledge, 1961), pp. 56–58.
19. Wittgenstein, *Tractatus*, p. 57.
20. Wittgenstein, *Tractatus*, p. 58.

real. In chapter 2, I remarked that scientific realism and Berkelean idealism seem to be two hypotheses accounting for exactly the same empirical evidence. Wittgenstein is suggesting that realism and solipsism similarly coincide.

Anyway, because of such experiences as that of the eclipse, I do (sort of) understand what Schopenhauer means when he says that in certain kinds of aesthetic experience, one detaches (to some extent, anyway) from one's individual will: "[F]or that moment we are delivered from the miserable pressure of the will. We celebrate the Sabbath of the penal servitude of willing; the wheel of Ixion stands still."[21] The feeling of serenity I experienced watching the eclipse would be an example. I agree with Schopenhauer that such moments are essential to a complete human life. They seem to have metaphysical, as opposed to merely psychological, significance. What they reveal, however, is difficult to express. Schopenhauer seems to think it cannot be said; it must manifest itself.

However, there are other kinds of aesthetic experience. Consider, for example, the experience of beauty I have when performing a great choral work with the New Mexico Symphony Orchestra Chorus. These are the aesthetic experiences I live for, the most gratifying parts of my life, and they do not involve anything like the sense of peace I felt so intensely watching the eclipse. When I am singing, I feel immersed in something that expresses the very nature of emotion. This is a far cry from leaving the will behind altogether.

The kind of aesthetic experience that stirs up emotions, rather than quieting them, seems altogether the most common. Even looking at a peaceful painting, or singing or listening to a gentle, soothing piece of music, is inaccurately described as involving a quieting of emotions. Rather, some emotions are violent and disturbing, whereas other emotions are peaceful and tranquil. Different works of art touch and amplify different emotions. A sort of catharsis may occur, so that one feels purged of emotion later, but during the aesthetic experience itself, the will is not abandoned but stimulated.

Schopenhauer insists, however, that not only does the appreciator of art experience will-less peace, such a will-less state is also achieved by the artist himself when creating or performing. This, too, seems wrong. Undoubtedly, when one is in the process of creating art, or performing music or drama, one enters a psychological

21. *WWR*, vol. 1, p. 196.

"flow" state in which one loses track of time, forgets to eat, does not even realize one is hungry, forgets daily responsibilities, and so forth. Perhaps this is what Schopenhauer is talking about. This is inaccurately described, however, as a will-less state. Rather, the artist is in the grip of a peculiarly intense kind of will—the will to create or express something true.

Schopenhauer finds it necessary to explain at some length that the artist begins with the Idea, not the concept. The distinction between Idea and concept is evidently important to Schopenhauer, and he struggles to make it clear. Imagine, for example, one of Leonardo's drawings of a horse. The drawing depicts, according to Schopenhauer, the Idea of a horse, not any individual horse, and not the concept of a horse.[22] The Idea is a real grade of the Will's objectification, a force of nature, known through perception. The concept is a definition or word or classification made by cognition or intellect, for purposes of rational thought. Concepts fall under the Principle of Sufficient Reason; Ideas are outside the Principle of Sufficient Reason. The concept contains only what we put into it; the Idea is inexhaustible in content.

The literary arts (e.g., poetry, drama, and fiction) have the same aim as the plastic arts, according to Schopenhauer—depiction of the perceptually intuited Ideas—but they must communicate the Ideas through concepts.[23] Tragedy is the summit of literary art because it describes the terrible side of life, thereby getting at the essence of reality:

> The unspeakable pain, the wretchedness and misery of mankind, the triumph of wickedness, the scornful mastery of chance, and the irretrievable fall of the just and the innocent are all here presented to us; and here is to be found a significant hint as to the nature of the world and of existence. It is the antagonism of the will with itself which is here most completely unfolded at the highest grade of its objectivity.[24]

Tragedy often pursues its practical end (to be a "quieter of the will") by depicting its heroes willingly giving up life; here Schopenhauer speaks of Hamlet.[25]

22. While the example of a Leonardo horse sketch is my own, Schopenhauer makes these points in *WWR*, vol. 1, p. 233.
23. *WWR*, vol. 1, pp. 242–243; see also vol. 2, pp. 424–438.
24. *WWR*, vol. 1, p. 253.
25. *WWR*, vol. 1, p. 253.

The artist intuits rather than explicitly understands what he is trying to express. He works instinctively, guided by the unconscious, from feeling, not from thought. This is all part of working from the Idea rather than from the concept, according to Schopenhauer. Most of what passes for art in any given age is but imitation, produced by frauds and sham artists, based on the concept rather than on the Idea. Only a few vital works really express the Idea, and these works speak to every age.[26]

In his struggle to differentiate Idea from concept, Schopenhauer is running into a familiar problem: his inability to decide whether, or to what extent, the Ideas are mind independent. Schopenhauer's attempt to distinguish the aims of art and science illustrates this same flaw. He says that science is confined to the study of individuals and their relations, within the bounds of the Principle of Sufficient Reason.[27] Art, by contrast, involves a way of considering things independently of the Principle of Sufficient Reason; it gets us to the Ideas, which are beyond the Principle of Sufficient Reason.[28]

Perhaps Schopenhauer should have said that classification systems are invented, but the divisions they mark out are perfectly real. Insofar as art gets at these real divisions in nature, its aim is the same as one of the aims of science. In accordance with such a view, Schopenhauer opines that art *shows* what science *says*. This latter claim is in tension with Schopenhauer's notion that art shows what can't be said.

This same kind of tension in Schopenhauer's aesthetics is brought out by the following peculiar quotation. Discussing aesthetic contemplation, Schopenhauer says: "[A]s pure subject of knowing, delivered from the miserable self, we become entirely one with [the objects].... Then the world as representation alone remains; the world as will has disappeared."[29]

Will is supposed to be the inner nature of the world; this is Schopenhauer's great teaching. He tells us that artistic experience is supposed to have metaphysical significance precisely because it reveals this inner nature of things.[30] Yet, in the quotation just given we encounter the assertion that artistic experience reveals not the world as will, but the world as representation. Well, which is it?

26. *WWR*, vol. 1, pp. 234–236; see also p. 182.
27. *WWR*, vol. 1, pp. 177, 185.
28. *WWR*, vol. 1, p. 178.
29. *WWR*, vol. 1, p. 199.
30. *WWR*, vol. 1, p. 222.

I believe Schopenhauer was confused and conflicted with regard to what, exactly, art shows. This parallels his conflict with regard to whether the Platonic Forms are phenomenal or noumenal.

Schopenhauer's Theory of Music in Particular

According to Schopenhauer, music manages to depict the Will itself, rather than any of the Platonic Forms that objectify or represent the Will. Instead of being a picture of a representation, music is a picture of reality itself. As Schopenhauer puts it:

> [Music] stands quite apart from all the others. In it we do not recognize the copy, the repetition, of any Idea of the inner nature of the world.... [W]e must attribute to music a far more serious and profound significance that refers to the innermost being of the world and of our own self.... [M]usic is by no means like the other arts, namely a copy of the Ideas, but *a copy of the will itself*, the objectivity of which are the Ideas.[31]

Leibniz allegedly said that music is an unconscious exercise in arithmetic in which the mind does not know it is counting.[32] Leibniz was evidently a mere listener, and not a performer, since anyone who plays or sings at a level beyond the elementary must count consciously.[33] Or, perhaps Leibniz was not thinking about the beat—maybe he just meant that music constitutes a complex, mathematically interesting structure. Putting that aside, however, Schopenhauer transforms Leibniz's remark into the following: music is an unconscious exercise in metaphysics in which the mind does not know it is philosophizing.[34] Music, rather than depicting any of the Platonic Forms or Ideas, depicts the thing in itself and is thus analogous to the whole world as representation:

> [W]e can regard the phenomenal world, or nature, and music as two different expressions of the same thing.... [M]usic differs from all the other arts by the fact that it is not a copy of the phenomenon, or,

31. *WWR*, vol. 1, pp. 256–257.

32. Quoted by Schopenhauer in *WWR*, vol. 1, p. 256.

33. It is worth noting here that Schopenhauer was himself an accomplished musician. He played the flute, favoring the compositions of Rossini and Mozart. See the biography of Schopenhauer by Rudiger Safranski, *Schopenhauer and the Wild Years of Philosophy*, trans. Ewald Osers (Cambridge: Harvard University Press, 1989).

34. *WWR*, vol. 1, p. 264.

more exactly, of the will's adequate objectivity, but is directly a copy of the will itself, and therefore expresses the metaphysical to everything physical in the world, the thing-in-itself to every phenomenon. Accordingly, we could just as well call the world embodied music as embodied will.[35]

Schopenhauer is trying to solve an aesthetic and metaphysical mystery: What is music about? It is clear to anyone who appreciates music that music is meaningful, but what does it mean? Every other art (except architecture, perhaps) obviously depicts something, but pure music, devoid of lyrics, has no obvious representational content at all. It is just patterns of sounds, of different frequencies and timbres, arranged according to mathematically expressible intervals and rhythms. Yet, music communicates something in and of itself. Any lyrics that may be set to it are secondary and dispensable. It already means what it means independently of the words, which may suit it well or badly.[36]

The most obvious answer as to what music represents seems to be emotion or feeling. Music has a notorious capacity to express and enhance moods and passions. There is happy music, sad music, exciting music, tranquil music. Just as a person's desires build over time, encountering obstacles and frustrations, often reaching a fevered pitch before being satisfied, music builds harmonic tensions and discords and then resolves them. The dynamic level of sound moves from very soft (*pianissimo*) up to very loud (*fortissimo*), and down again, with all levels in between. This, too, has an analogy with emotion. A soft passage of music may express a mild emotion or an intense emotion that is merely suppressed. Loud music may represent a particularly vehement emotion or the release of any feeling long bottled up. Schopenhauer chooses music's analogy with feeling as the key to its meaning:

[T]he nature of man consists in the fact that his will strives, is satisfied, strives anew, and so on and on; in fact his happiness and wellbeing consist only in the transition from desire to satisfaction, and from this to a fresh desire.... [M]elody expresses the many different

35. *WWR*, vol. 1, pp. 262–263.
36. See *WWR*, vol. 2, pp. 448–449: "The words are and remain for the music a foreign extra of secondary value, as the effect of the tones is incomparably more powerful, more infallible, and more rapid than that of the words.... [I]t might perhaps appear more suitable for the text to be written for the music than for the music to be composed for the text."

forms of the will's efforts, but also its satisfaction by ultimately finding again a harmonious interval, and still more the keynote.... [A]s rapid
transition from wish to satisfaction and from this to a new wish are
happiness and well-being, so rapid melodies without great deviations
are cheerful. Slow melodies that strike painful discords, and wind
back to the keynote only through many bars, are sad, on the analogy
of delayed and hard-won satisfaction.[37]

It is well known that pieces in a major key seem to express positive feelings, whereas pieces in a minor key express anxiety, tension,
or sadness. It is hard to understand why this should be the case, and
Schopenhauer acknowledges the mystery: "[H]ow marvelous is the
effect of *minor* and *major*! How astonishing that the change of half a
tone, the entrance of a minor third instead of a major, at once and
inevitably forces on us an anxious and painful feeling, from which
we are again delivered just as instantaneously by the major!"[38]

Though the exact relationship of human emotions to various
features of music cannot always be clearly explained, the general
affinity between music and emotion, once it is pointed out, is so
obvious that no one questions it. Schopenhauer takes the essence
of a human being to be will, which for Schopenhauer is not rational but emotional. So, according to Schopenhauer, music expresses
the inner nature of man. The essence of man is the same as the
essence of everything; all the forces of nature are the same thing we
experience in ourselves as will. Therefore, music expresses the inner
nature of everything.

Schopenhauer draws an analogy between four-part choral har-
mony (soprano, alto, tenor, bass) and his own scheme of four levels within the world as representation. The bass corresponds to the
basic physical forces, such as gravity and electromagnetism. The
tenor corresponds to plant life. The alto corresponds to the animal.
Finally, the soprano (usually carrying the melody) corresponds to
humanity, the highest grade of the Will's objectification.[39] I must
admit I find this charming, though it is perhaps excessively fanciful.

Schopenhauer seems right when he says that music expresses
not only human emotion, but the inner nature of everything. If
indeed motivation is causality seen from within, then our emotions
are examples of the same forces, the same buildups and releases of

37. *WWR*, vol. 1, p. 260.
38. *WWR*, vol. 1, p. 261.
39. *WWR*, vol. 2, p. 447.

energy, that occur throughout nature, both in the parts we think of as living and the parts we think of as nonliving. Any music that may be interpreted in terms of human feelings, then, could just as well be interpreted in terms of animals or plants, or physical/geological features such as rocks, rivers, and volcanoes.

Here is Schopenhauer in his own words:

> [A] symphony of Beethoven presents us with the greatest confusion which yet has the most perfect order as its foundation; with the most vehement conflict which is transformed the next moment into the most beautiful harmony. It is "the discordant concord of the world," a true and complete picture of the nature of the world, which rolls on in the boundless confusion of innumerable forms, and maintains itself by constant destruction. But at the same time, all the human passions and emotions speak from this symphony; joy, grief, love, hatred, terror, hope, and so on in innumerable shades, yet all, as it were, only in the abstract and without any particularization; it is their mere form without the material, like a mere spirit world without matter. We certainly have an inclination to realize it while we listen, to clothe it in the imagination with flesh and bone, and to see in it all the different scenes of life and nature. On the whole, however, this does not promote an understanding or enjoyment of it, but rather gives it a strange and arbitrary addition. It is therefore better to interpret it purely and in its immediacy.[40]

This seems exactly right. One person might listen to the second movement of Beethoven's Ninth Symphony and envision some scene of human endeavor and action; another might see in his mind galloping and jumping horses; a third might imagine a rapid river tumbling over rocks and falls. The characters involved in the imagery don't matter. What matters is that the music is obviously about the release and expression of great energy (Beethoven marks the second movement of the Ninth *molto vivace* and *presto*). Wherever and however such energy release might occur in nature, this music depicts it.

What seems wrong, in Schopenhauer's account of music, is the view that music differs from other fine arts in its ability to depict ultimate reality, beyond the forms of representation imposed by the human mind. In my view, *all* the fine arts do that. The fine arts other than music, however, are confined to depicting this or that

40. *WWR*, vol. 2, p. 450.

particular natural force or form. Music manages to be about all natural forms and forces at once, and none in particular.

The Character of Genius

When Schopenhauer speaks of the nature of genius, his remarks are a curious combination of insight, error, and contradiction.[41] The genius sees beyond the individual objects he actually encounters in experience to the eternal types they exemplify. He is less concerned with his own personal needs and welfare than the average man. "Whereas to the ordinary man his faculty of knowledge is a lamp that lights his path, to the man of genius it is the sun that reveals the world."[42] Genius is opposed to prudence. "A *prudent* man will not be a genius insofar as and while he is prudent; and a *genius* will not be prudent insofar as and while he is a genius."[43] Accordingly, the productions of genius are *not useful*; this is the mark of their nobility.[44] Geniuses can exhibit several weaknesses that are akin to mental illness, such as obsessiveness.[45]

According to Schopenhauer, any advance beyond the norm in intellect already predisposes a person to mental illness,[46] and a genius is two-thirds intellect with one-third will, whereas an ordinary person is two-thirds will and one-third intellect.[47] Because of the predominance of intellect over will in his psyche, the genius is able to achieve a state of pure perception where the intellect is no longer serving the will (I have already discussed how problematic this is).

Despite possessing the capacity for disinterested contemplation, and the predominance of intellect over will, the genius tends to be

41. Schopenhauer discusses the nature of genius primarily in *WWR*, vol. 1, pp. 184–194.

42. *WWR*, vol. 1, p. 188.

43. *WWR*, vol. 1, pp. 189–190.

44. *WWR*, vol. 2, p. 388.

45. *WWR*, vol. 2, pp. 387–389. In general, Schopenhauer's speculations on the nature of "madness" exhibit the same mixture of insight and error as his speculations on the nature of genius. See *WWR*, vol. 1, pp. 192–194, and vol. 2, pp. 399–402. Anyone who has read Freud will be struck by how much Schopenhauer's thoughts here evidently influenced Freud's own explorations.

46. *WWR*, vol. 1, p. 191.

47. *WWR*, vol. 2, p. 377.

a passionate, tormented individual, capable of violent emotions and often prone to melancholy. Schopenhauer sees the apparent contradiction involved in this claim and attempts to ameliorate it as follows: the cause of the genius's passionate nature is not any weakness in his intellect, but "unusual energy of...will."[48] With regard to the depression often accompanying genius, Schopenhauer notes, "[T]he brighter the intellect enlightening the will-to-live, the more distinctly does it perceive the wretchedness of its condition."[49]

I find it odd that Schopenhauer pinpoints predominance of intellect over will and the capacity for passionless intellect as hallmarks of genius. It seems to me, rather, that geniuses possess a vehement desire to know and to express the truth, in addition to the intellectual ability to find out the truth. They have a *will* to match their strong intellect, and that *will* is directed toward the same end as the intellect: truth. Geniuses are just as much predominantly willing creatures as the rest of us, but their strongest desire is for something eternal, beyond the satisfaction of mundane needs and personal desires. We might call this strong desire the will-to-truth. Above I mentioned the capacity to enter a psychological "flow" state in which the will-to-truth predominates over all other forms of willing; everyday needs and desires are forgotten in a frenzy of creativity. Perhaps geniuses excel over the rest of us in their capacity to enter such a state, largely because of their stronger will-to-truth.

Schopenhauer evidently does not believe that there can be such a thing as a *scientific* genius; geniuses are always artists. This is because science is confined to the study of individual things and their relations, within the sphere of the Principle of Sufficient Reason, and is blind to the Forms or Ideas.[50] I have already remarked that this strikes me as wrong, since science seeks to classify things according to their essential types. Furthermore, most of the apt anecdotes Schopenhauer offers about the nature of artistic geniuses (inattention to personal needs, obsessiveness, etc.) seem to apply equally well to scientific geniuses. Great scientists, like great artists, seem prone to intuitive leaps of insight that come from the unconscious (e.g., the structure of the benzene ring came to August Kekulé in a dream; a dream was also the source of Dmitri Mendeleyev's idea for

48. *WWR*, vol. 1, p. 190.
49. *WWR*, vol. 2, p. 383.
50. *WWR*, vol. 1, pp. 184–185.

the periodic table of the elements). Perhaps scientists are less prone to melancholy and violent emotions than artists—but even if this is true, I doubt it indicates any essential difference between scientists and artists in respect of their genius.

Incredibly, Schopenhauer asserts that geniuses have no inclination toward mathematics:

> The disinclination of men of genius to direct their attention to the content of the principle of sufficient reason will show itself first in regard to the ground of being, as a disinclination for mathematics.... [T]he logical procedure of mathematics will be repugnant to genius, for it obscures real insight and does not satisfy it.... Experience has also confirmed that men of great artistic genius have no aptitude for mathematics; no man was ever very distinguished in both at the same time.[51]

Though it may be true that great mathematicians and great artists are exclusive classes, artists (greater and lesser) must have *some* appreciation of math. Musicians have to count their rhythms, and there are mathematical principles to perspective drawing, for example. Furthermore, just as most of Schopenhauer's observations about the character of genius apply to great scientists, they also apply to great mathematicians. Indeed, an ability to intuit something real and eternal beyond the visible world seems characteristic of a mathematician. Schopenhauer's idea that mathematics is strictly concerned with the "world as representation" and not with the nature of things in themselves appears wrong-headed—and Schopenhauer, as an admirer of Plato, should have appreciated just how wrong it seems.

Schopenhauer's tiresome misogyny surfaces in his claim that a woman cannot be a genius.[52] It seems never to have occurred to Schopenhauer that the paucity of female geniuses in history might be accounted for by a lack of opportunities afforded to women, rather than by some deficiency in the essential nature of women. He does note, correctly, that geniuses are childlike in many respects— they are, in some ways, people who never grow up, who continue to ask naive questions and refuse to adopt conventional ways of looking at things.[53] Again, however, this applies to a scientist (Albert Einstein) as much as it applies to a painter (Pablo Picasso), a poet (Walt Whitman, Emily Dickinson), or an author (George Eliot).

51. *WWR*, vol. 1, pp. 188–189.
52. *WWR*, vol. 2, p. 392.
53. *WWR*, vol. 2, p. 395.

Summary of My Suggestions

Let me extract from Schopenhauer's aesthetics the elements worth keeping, and reject or correct the rest.

Schopenhauer is right that there exists a peculiar, transcendent sort of aesthetic experience in which the world and our individual wills seem to stop for a few blessed moments, leaving us with a sense of holy peace. During such experiences, we at least come close to being "the clear eye of the world,"[54] seeing how things are without wishing for things to be different. This kind of experience does indeed seem to have metaphysical significance, and it does give us a glimpse of something that might be called "enlightenment."

He is also right that music, among the fine arts, is special. It is special, however, not because it alone among the arts penetrates beyond the representation (*all* arts penetrate beyond the representation) but because it depicts the essence of all the various forces and forms of nature, whereas the other arts must depict particular forms and forces.

Schopenhauer confuses and obscures the crucial point that art and music are significant precisely because they offer us insight into the true nature of things. Schopenhauer's unfortunate anti-realism gets in the way and makes him say that the fine arts (other than music) can only depict something not quite real, something made up by the human mind. The same point applies to Schopenhauer's evaluation of science. Science, philosophy, and art, I believe, all have the same goal: to get at mind-independent reality. Geniuses are found not just among artists, but among scientists, philosophers, and mathematicians. What distinguishes the genius from the rest of us is not only an extraordinary intellect, but an extraordinary will to perceive and express the truth.

Furthermore, the most common type of aesthetic experience is not the transcendent kind that quiets the will, but rather an immersion into, and being carried by, our feelings. (As a lover of music, Schopenhauer should have realized this.) Since these feelings are exemplary of the force or causal power that constitutes the inner nature of everything, this kind of experience, too, has metaphysical significance.

---

54. Schopenhauer uses the phrase "the clear eye of the world" to characterize "the pure knowing subject" in *WWR*, vol. I, p. 186.

CHAPTER FIVE

Pessimism, Depression, and Salvation

We have seen, in previous chapters, that Schopenhauer was torn between anti-realism and realism. This chapter shows that this conflict parallels another conflict in Schopenhauer's psyche: he was also torn between what he calls "affirmation of the will" and "denial of the will." While he officially identifies the latter as the way to "salvation," his actual life shows that he followed the other path and, indeed, found at least some peace and satisfaction through self-discovery and self-expression.

Should we heed what Schopenhauer says, or look at what his life shows? Both, I believe. Persons capable of enlightenment in the sense of extinguishing the ego are extremely rare. For the majority of human beings gifted enough to reach what Schopenhauer calls "self-knowledge,"[1] it is affirmation of the will, through creative self-realization, that beckons as the way to a life containing enough joy to make it worthwhile.

Schopenhauer, of course, denies that life is *ever* worthwhile. This is his famous pessimism. We shall consider to what extent it is objectively justifiable. We shall also look into what exactly is meant by "salvation."

---

1. Schopenhauer seems to include in "self-knowledge" both the philosophical realization that all things are manifestations of one great Will, and the practical development of "acquired character"—the personal knowledge of who one is, of what one wants and doesn't want, of what one can and can't do.

Recall that in chapter 4 I noted that the state of "will-less contemplation" allegedly achieved by the artistic genius, and by the true appreciator of art, ought not to be possible, on Schopenhauer's own terms. Likewise, the complete denial of the will-to-live allegedly achieved by saints ought not to be possible, on Schopenhauer's own terms. If will is the very essence of existence, how is it possible to transcend it? Schopenhauer's "single thought" undoubtedly contains more than a mystical intuition of the sameness of the inner nature of all things. The "one thought" also includes the paradox that in some human beings, it is possible for the will to transcend itself. These rare individuals manage to "stop the world," to use a quasi-Buddhist expression popular in my youth. This ought not to be possible; yet, according to Schopenhauer, it is.

Pessimism as a Philosophical Orientation

The ancient Greek god Silenus supposedly taught that life is not worth living. According to mythology, Silenus told King Midas that the best of all possible things is never to be born at all, and that if one is unlucky enough to be born, the best thing is to die soon.

This teaching of Silenus is often quoted as the essence of pessimism and is echoed by writers such as Sophocles:

> Never to have been born is best,
> But if we must see the light, the next best
> Is quickly returning whence we came.
> When youth departs, with all its follies,
> Who does not stagger under evils? Who escapes them?[2]

Of course, the thought, "I would have been better off if I had never been born," is paradoxical. If I had never been born, there would have been no "I" to have been better off. Is it paradoxical merely to *wish* one had never been born? If so, the paradox is not obvious. Many of us do have this wish, from time to time.

It has occurred to me that whereas we celebrate birth and mourn death, perhaps we have it backward. Since life inevitably contains much suffering, and death is the cessation of all suffering, maybe we

---

2. Sophocles, *Oedipus at Colonus*, lines 1224–1231. Quoted in David Benatar, *Better Never to Have Been: The Harm of Coming into Existence* (Oxford: Oxford University Press, 2006), p. 18.

ought to weep when a child is born and celebrate when someone dies.[3] Such a thought certainly occurred to Schopenhauer. He says: "[A]s regards the life of the individual, every life-history is a history of suffering, for, as a rule, every life is a continual series of mishaps great and small.... [A]t the end of his life, no man, if he be sincere and at the same time in possession of his faculties, will ever wish to go through it again. Rather than this, he will much prefer to choose complete non-existence."[4]

Schopenhauer also reflects that the instinct toward self-preservation found in all living things cannot have its origin in knowledge and experience, since "the objective value of life is very uncertain, and it remains at least doubtful whether existence is to be preferred to non-existence; in fact, if experience and reflection have their say, non-existence must certainly win. If we knocked on the graves and asked the dead whether they would like to rise again, they would shake their heads."[5] He approvingly notes that this was Socrates' position in the *Apology*, and reports that "even the cheerful and amiable Voltaire" believed life to be a bad joke, not obviously preferable to complete nothingness.[6]

At the core of Schopenhauer's pessimism is the thought that there is no final satisfaction for the endless desire or striving that constitutes the inner nature of everything:

[T]he will dispenses entirely with an ultimate aim and object. It always strives, because striving is its sole nature, to which no

---

3. It might seem that this thought implies that killing someone is therefore (always) doing her a favor, so killing is never wrong. Most of us don't want to draw such an inference. A person's life is her property, and it is wrong to deprive someone of her property. What about abortion? If we grant that a fetus does not yet possess an independent life of its own, perhaps the moral rightness of abortion *does* follow from pessimism. By aborting a fetus, one saves it from the pointless and unredeemed suffering that is life. Abortion is thus a deeply moral act. (I recall here an old feminist adage: "If men could get pregnant, abortion would be a sacrament.") There is a haunting scene in Woody Allen's film *Match Point* (2005) in which the main character, who has murdered his pregnant mistress along with an innocent woman, is confronted with the ghosts of his victims. While his justifications for killing the two women are clearly in bad faith, when confronted with the question, "What about your unborn child?" he cites the wisdom of Silenus: "Never to be born is best." Is this bad faith, or the truth?

4. Schopenhauer, *The World as Will and Representation* (hereafter *WWR*), vol. 1, p. 324.

5. *WWR*, vol. 2, p. 465.

6. *WWR*, vol. 2, p. 465.

attained goal can put an end....We saw this in the simplest of all
natural phenomena, namely gravity, which does not cease to strive
and press toward an extensionless central point, whose attainment
would be the annihilation of itself and of matter; it would not cease,
even if the whole universe were already rolled into a ball....[T]he
existence of the plant is just such a restless, never-satisfied striving,
a ceaseless activity through higher and higher forms, till the final
point, the seed, becomes anew a starting-point, and this is repeated
ad infinitum....We have long since recognized this striving that constitutes the kernel and in-itself of everything, as the same thing
that in us...is called *will*. We call its hindrance through an obstacle
placed between it and its temporary goal, *suffering*; its attainment of
the goal, on the other hand, we call *satisfaction*, well-being, happiness....[A]ll striving springs from want or deficiency, from dissatisfaction with one's own state or condition, and is therefore suffering
so long as it is not satisfied. No satisfaction, however, is lasting; on
the contrary, it is always merely the starting-point of a fresh striving....[T]hat there is no ultimate aim of striving means that there is
no measure or end of suffering.[7]

Schopenhauer goes on to say that whereas the suffering of nonliving
systems and plants is unconscious, suffering becomes conscious in animals, and ever more acute in more complex and cognitively advanced
animals. In human beings suffering reaches its apex, and the more
gifted the person, the more acute the suffering:

[I]n proportion as knowledge attains to distinctness, consciousness
is enhanced, pain also increases, and consequently reaches its highest degree in man; and all the more, the more distinctly he knows,
and the more intelligent he is. The person in whom genius is to be
found suffers most of all....I understand and here use that saying in
Ecclesiastes, "He that increaseth knowledge increaseth sorrow."[8]

From such premises Schopenhauer draws the conclusion that in
its essence *all life is suffering*.[9] One may object that the argument is
fallacious, since properly speaking the word "suffering" denotes a
state of pain, and most lives, most of the time, are not positively
painful. There is an overall pleasantness to the recurrence of mundane desires, together with the ability to satisfy them, even if the
satisfaction is never lasting and a new desire always comes along

7. *WWR*, vol. 1, pp. 308–309.
8. *WWR*, vol. 1, p. 310.
9. *WWR*, vol. 1, p. 310.

to replace the old one.[10] There is also, occasionally, the great happiness of the fulfillment of a large goal, a long-term desire. Such happiness admittedly doesn't last, but these moments of triumph are still sweet and made sweeter by the difficulty of their attainment.[11] In addition, as many philosophers have noted, there is a kind of pleasure, peculiarly solid and durable, that comes from learning and understanding.

Even though life can be pleasant for long stretches of time and contains its consolations and exquisitely fine moments, nobody escapes positive pain. Disease, defect, loneliness, injury, sorrow, heartbreak, fear, defeat, humiliation—all these evils, and more, are part of everyone's life. If one if "lucky" enough to reach old age, one faces perhaps the worst evils of all—bodily decrepitude, mental deterioration, loss of autonomy and independence. Thus, even if it is not the case that life is suffering in its very essence, life inevitably *contains* suffering. Does the pleasurable side of life balance out the painful side and make life overall worth living, or does the pain rather cancel out the pleasure, making life overall a bad bargain? Schopenhauer argues for the latter, pessimistic conclusion. He notes that even among those who live in tolerably fortunate circumstances, their good fortune itself ironically gives rise to a new evil, boredom:

[A]s soon as want and suffering give man a relaxation, boredom is at once so near that he necessarily requires diversion and amusement. The striving after existence is what occupies all living things, and keeps them in motion. When existence is assured to them, they do not know what to do with it. Therefore the second thing that sets them in motion is the effort to get rid of the burden of existence, to make it no longer felt, "to kill time," in other words to escape from boredom. Accordingly we see that almost all men, secure from

10. Even Schopenhauer admits, "For desire and satisfaction to follow each other at not too short and not too long intervals, reduces the suffering occasioned by both to the smallest amount, and constitutes the happiest life" (*WWR*, vol. 1, p. 314). Note the analogy with happy melodies in music, of which Schopenhauer says, "[A]s rapid transition from wish to satisfaction and from this to a new wish are happiness and well-being, so rapid melodies without great deviations are cheerful" (p. 260).

11. Again, note the analogy with music: "Slow melodies that strike painful discords and wind back to the keynote only through many bars, are sad, on the analogy of delayed and hard-won satisfaction.... [T]he *allegro maestoso* in great phrases, long passages, and wide deviations expresses a greater, nobler effort towards a distant goal, and its final attainment" (*WWR*, vol. 1, pp. 260–261).

wants and cares, are now a burden to themselves, after having finally cast off all other burdens....Boredom is anything but an evil to be thought of lightly; ultimately it depicts on the countenance real despair.[12]

Mild distress, temporary relief from mild distress, boredom, and temporary relief from boredom constitute the great part of human existence for the most fortunate. The less fortunate have it even worse. Schopenhauer asks us to think about the lives of most people, throughout most of human history, and to reflect that their lives have been (to borrow Hobbes's adjectives) nasty, brutish, and short. Even now, unimaginable numbers of people live in misery with little or no relief:

> If we were to conduct the most hardened and callous optimist through hospitals, infirmaries, operating theaters, through prisons, torture-chambers, and slave-hovels, over battlefields, to places of execution; if we were to open to him all the dark abodes of misery, where it shuns the gaze of cold curiosity, and finally were we to allow him to glance into the dungeon of Ugolino where prisoners starved to death, he too would certainly see in the end what kind of world is this "best of all possible worlds." For whence did Dante get the material for his hell, if not from this actual world of ours?[13]

Schopenhauer notes that anything good and fine in this world is always the exception, never the rule:

> [E]verything better struggles through only with difficulty; what is noble and wise very rarely makes its appearance, becomes effective, or meets with a hearing, but the absurd and perverse in the realm of thought, the dull and tasteless in the sphere of art, and the wicked and fraudulent in the sphere of action, really assert a supremacy that is disturbed only by brief interruptions.... [E]verything excellent or admirable is always only an exception, one case in millions.[14]

---

12. *WWR*, vol. 1, p. 313. Schopenhauer's musical analogy for boredom is the monotonous melody where a single note is repeated over and over (p. 260). While boredom is not itself a mental illness, it is surely one of the causes of many kinds of mental illness, including depression and substance abuse. I am reminded here of Freud's idea that in proportion as men have the external comforts of civilization, they suffer the internal discomforts of mental illness. Conquering nature, making life more comfortable and secure, does not eliminate suffering. Instead, new forms of suffering arise to replace the original forms. See Freud, *Civilization and Its Discontents*, trans. James Strachey (New York: W. W. Norton and Co., 1961).

13. *WWR*, vol. 1, p. 325.

14. *WWR*, vol. 1, p. 324.

Thus, Schopenhauer's conclusion is that the bad clearly outweighs the good, both in the case of individual lives and in the case of human life in general, if one actually bothers to think about it. Schopenhauer says that optimism (the notion that human life is a good thing, with happiness as its object) is "a really *wicked* way of thinking" that "makes a mockery of the unspeakable suffering of mankind."[15]

An additional aspect of Schopenhauer's pessimism is his awareness of the cyclical and ultimately futile nature of all things. He clearly agrees with the gloomy old preacher of Ecclesiastes that all endeavor is ultimately in vain and that there is nothing new under the sun. This, of course, is just another way of stating the point that the will can achieve no lasting satisfaction, but such passages as the following have a peculiar resonance:

> It is really incredible how meaningless and insignificant when seen from without, and how dull and senseless when felt from within, is the course of life of the great majority of men. It is weary longing and worrying, a dreamlike staggering through the four ages of life to death, accompanied by a series of trivial thoughts. They are like clockwork that is wound up and goes without knowing why. Every time a man is begotten and born the clock of human life is wound up anew, to repeat once more its same old tune that has already been played innumerable times, movement by movement and measure by measure, with insignificant variations. Every individual, every human apparition and its course of life, is only one more short dream of the endless spirit of nature, of the persistent will-to-live.[16]

I can certainly recall having had the thought, fairly early in life, "What's the point of it all? Why should I go through the dreary, mind-numbing torture of public school, get some dreary, mind-numbing job, get married, and have children? So my children can go through the dreary, mind-numbing torture of public school, get dreary, mind-numbing jobs, get married, and have more children...and so on, *ad indefinitum*?" Just as Schopenhauer says, there is no point. Nature has no reason. It just wants to make more of itself, to repeat the cycle. Most people tread the well-trodden path laid down for them by countless previous generations, making their living and having their own children, propelled by want and necessity and blind sexual instinct, without really thinking much about it at all. The Will that drives all this does not care about the individual

15. *WWR*, vol. I, p. 326.
16. *WWR*, vol. I, pp. 321–322.

and his suffering at all. If it cares about anything, this Will cares only about perpetuating the species.

Schopenhauer is deeply opposed to the historical optimism of Hegel, who believed that human history is progressive, heading toward something. Rather, says Schopenhauer, human history shows us the same old patterns, being repeated over and over again:

> [H]istory is untruthful not only in its arrangement, but also in its very nature, since, speaking of mere individuals and particular events, it always pretends to relate something different, whereas from beginning to end it constantly repeats only the same thing under a different name and in a different cloak. The true philosophy of history thus consists in the insight that, in spite of all these endless changes and their chaos and confusion, we yet always have before us only the same, identical, unchangeable essence, acting in the same way today as it did yesterday and always.[17]

There is an "inborn error" according to which we exist in order to be happy, and simple-minded philosophies and religions encourage this error. The illusion that social progress is really possible, that it is possible to make "a heaven here on earth" (as the Unitarians believe) is part of this error. Intelligent people, confronted with experience, soon find out that the world is *not* arranged so as to facilitate human happiness, but rather the contrary. The impossibility of eliminating poverty and misery in the world in general parallels the impossibility of achieving lasting happiness on an individual scale. Unproblematic progress, like lasting happiness, is simply *not in the nature of things*. This conflict of experience with received dogma is a source of perplexity and depression and is one aspect of the "riddle of the world." The deep teaching of the wisest philosophies and religions is that we exist in order to suffer; life is *not* a good thing, and we shall never by our puny efforts make it a good thing. Realizing that life is not good and that we were not meant to be happy is, accordingly, one aspect of the answer to the riddle, a step on the road to salvation.[18]

Optimism and Pessimism as Personality Traits

Often, when we use the word "pessimism," we don't mean any articulated philosophical orientation. Rather, we mean a general personality trait. In this sense, both pessimism and optimism seem to

---

17. *WWR*, vol. 2, p. 444.
18. *WWR*, vol. 2, pp. 634–635; see also pp. 638–639.

be general stances or sets of expectations people adopt toward the world. Pessimists focus on the negative aspects of life, expect things to turn out badly, and approach the world warily. Optimists emphasize the positive, expect things to go well, and approach the world with trust. Perhaps there are inborn, genetic tendencies contributing to the stance a given person adopts. Such inborn tendencies, if they exist, surely interact with life experience to produce the full-blown traits of optimism or pessimism.

Personality traits can turn into philosophical orientations when the possessors of these traits begin consciously and articulately to *theorize* about the world.

The Danger of the Attribution Fallacy

Social psychologists speak of the fundamental attribution fallacy. That's when we see our mistakes as a natural consequence of the situation we happen to be in ("*I* couldn't park *my* car very well because *the space* was too small") and others' failings as due to failings in them ("*You* couldn't park *your* car very well because *you* are an incompetent driver").

It is at least possible that pessimism and optimism, when they become articulate philosophical orientations, are both instances of the attribution fallacy. Pessimism seems to endow the world with evil motives: "The world is designed to frustrate us and succeeds more often than not." Optimism seems to endow the world with benevolence: "God's in his heaven and all's right with the world."[19] The truth may be that the world is neutral—neither malevolent nor benevolent—and *we* endow it with these properties according to the bent of our character and the course of our life-experience.

If being an optimist or a pessimist as an articulate philosophical orientation is a fallacy, it is a peculiarly difficult fallacy to correct. Can I help seeing the world the way I see it? Is it possible to be neither an optimist nor a pessimist and to regard the world neutrally? Personally, I am a pessimist, and I find it impossible to abandon this stance. The best I can do is to remind myself periodically that my view may be as distorted in its own way as that of the sunny optimist.

19. Robert Browning, whose poem *Pippa Passes* is the source of this famous line, was no optimist. The line is meant ironically. Thanks here to my late friend Paul A. Smith, who was an appreciative reader of both Browning and Schopenhauer.

Depression and the Psychological Roots
of Pessimism

Let us speak from now on of pessimism as an articulated philosophical orientation rather than a mere personality trait. Thoughtful
people have always recognized that there are some deep truths
embodied in pessimism. Why else would we respond as we do to
tragedy? When Hamlet or Lear soliloquizes about the pain and futil-
ity of existence, we know in our hearts that he speaks the truth (or
at least, one aspect of the truth). The book of Ecclesiastes and the
book of Job belong in the Bible because they also speak, or show,
great and inevitable truths: life always contains much suffering, the
bad probably outweighs the good, life is not fair, and there is no
satisfactory explanation for any of this other than *that's the way it is.*

Nevertheless, I have heard people say that Schopenhauer was
obviously mentally ill. "He would not have adopted such a grim
view of life unless he were depressed." This (fairly common) reaction
to the writings of the pessimistic philosopher raises several interesting questions: Is pessimism necessarily pathological, the deliverance
of a diseased mind? Did Schopenhauer suffer from depression? If he
did, does this cast doubt on the cogency of his arguments or the
truth of his conclusions? Most interesting of all: Is depression itself
one face of "the riddle of the world," the question that demands
"salvation" as its answer?

I do not believe that pessimism is necessarily pathological.
Suppose we define "pessimism" as the view that life contains more
unhappiness than happiness, and that some of this unhappiness is so
dreadful that a reasonable person would prefer nonexistence to having to endure it. It seems to me that this is objectively justified: the
facts support it. Of course, I *would* think that, because of the bent of
my personality, together with the danger of slipping into the attribution fallacy. But the question we want to consider here is: Does
a person have to be *sick*, mentally *ill*, in order to accept philosophical pessimism? I do not believe so. Many writers and thinkers generally acknowledged to be great have said (and shown) that life is
essentially terrible. If Schopenhauer was sick, then so were Socrates,
Sartre, Sophocles, Shakespeare, and many others whose names do
not begin with S.

One need not be depressed to accept pessimism. (Recall
Schopenhauer's own citation of Voltaire, a pessimist who was not

depressed.) Still, it seems likely that experience of depression might be a causal factor leading some people to become pessimists. Was Schopenhauer depressed?

There is evidence that Schopenhauer suffered from what would now be called "dysthymic disorder" (chronic bad mood),[20] manifesting itself as a general contrariness.

While I have chosen to use the word "dysthymic" to describe Schopenhauer, I am generally uncomfortable using today's psychiatric labels to characterize the personality traits and behavioral symptoms of persons in the past. This practice is anachronistic and ignores the fact, well established by recent philosophers, that various mental "disorders" are at least partially socially constructed entities. Different mental illnesses come and go in history, as if they were the creations of transient social conditions. Mental illnesses may even in some cases be invented by doctors, whose nonobjective "gaze" endows patients with imagined or expected symptoms. If we look at different periods in the history of psychiatry, we see that different "illnesses" have been widespread at different times. In Freud's day, for example, lots of women had "hysteria," and lots of men had "neurasthenia." Today, almost nobody shows the symptoms commonly seen in Freud's time, and other "mental illnesses," such as eating disorders and attention deficit disorder, are common. One fascinating aspect of this is that, because human beings are so vulnerable to the power of suggestion, patients often begin to exhibit precisely the symptoms the physician imagines or expects to see. For example, a patient might self-identify as "bipolar," with the encouragement of her physician, and go on to exhibit extreme mood swings. Another patient, told he has multiple personality disorder, might begin to act out manifestations of "alters," unconscious of any willful faking.[21] Another set of issues about the objectivity of mental illness arises because the psychiatric community today is under pressure from pharmaceutical companies to label all kinds of personality traits and life problems as "disorders," due to the fact

20. See *Diagnostic and Statistical Manual of Mental Disorders*, 4th ed., text revision (Washington, D.C.: American Psychiatric Association, 2000), sec. 300.4.

21. See Ian Hacking, *The Social Construction of What?* (Cambridge: Harvard University Press, 2001); and *Re-writing the Soul: Multiple Personality and the Sciences of Memory* (Princeton: Princeton University Press, 1995). See also Michel Foucault, *Madness and Civilization: A History of Insanity in the Age of Reason* (New York: Random House, 1965); and *The Birth of the Clinic: An Archaeology of Medical Perception* (New York: Random House, 1973). "Gaze" is a translation of one of Foucault's terms.

that pharmaceutical firms can make big money selling personality-altering and emotion-altering drugs.

Thoughtful, responsible psychiatrists and psychologists reserve the term "disorder" for conditions that substantially interfere with a patient's ability to realize life goals and carry out meaningful projects. Even under this definition, however, it is impossible to draw a clear line between disorders and features of character.

Whether or not Schopenhauer had a chronic personality disorder, other people typically found him unpleasant. Even his own mother, Joanna Schopenhauer (a novelist whose books were popular in their day), was reluctant to live with her son as an adult because of his dour demeanor.[22] She wrote to him as follows in 1807, when he was contemplating moving in with her in Weimar:

> I have always told you that you are very difficult to live with.... [S]o long as you are as you are, I would rather make any sacrifice than decide in favor of living together.... [T]hat which repels me from you lies not in your...inmost being but in your manner, your exterior, your views, your judgments, your habits....I cannot agree with you in anything that concerns the external world; moreover, your ill humor depresses me and upsets my serenity without helping you in the least.... [During a recent visit] I only breathed freely again when you were gone, because your presence, your complaints about inevitable things, your scowling face, the bizarre judgments uttered by you like oracular pronouncements not permitting any kind of objection, oppressed me.[23]

One must agree with Joanna herself that this unflattering portrait of young Arthur does not show his truest character. Deep inside, Schopenhauer was a tender-hearted man, loving and deeply hungry for love, but this very sensitivity led him to be wounded and perplexed by life and the world. Thus came about the chronic, mild depression that manifested itself as irascibility and negativity.

22. In investigating Schopenhauer's family background, one comes to see why Schopenhauer believed intellect was inherited from the mother and character from the father. He was taking his own case and applying it to the world in general (just as Freud was later to do with certain features of his personal psychological development, e.g., the "castration complex"). Schopenhauer's father had a depressive, introverted character like his son, but a rather commonplace mind concerned primarily with money and commerce. Schopenhauer's mother, Joanna, was an extremely intelligent woman but, unlike her son, was optimistic and sociable.

23. Quoted in Rudiger Safranski, *Schopenhauer and the Wild Years of Philosophy*, trans. Ewald Osers (Cambridge: Harvard University Press, 1989), p. 92.

A famous anecdote reinforces the impression of Schopenhauer as a crabby and unpleasant person. Allegedly, he assaulted his landlady on one occasion, giving her a shove that led to her falling and being injured. This incident gave rise to a lawsuit that plagued Schopenhauer for years.

In addition to his general grouchiness, there is further evidence that Schopenhauer suffered a few episodes of full-blown, major depression. When Arthur was in his late teens, his father was found dead, an apparent suicide.[24] In the aftermath of this traumatic event, Arthur himself wrote, "[M]y sadness deepened to such an extent that it was scarcely distinguishable from real melancholia."[25] One can see that this early depression was precipitated by conflicted feelings. As long as Arthur's father was alive, Arthur felt obligated to follow his father's wishes and pursue a career in business. It was his father's suicide that freed Arthur to follow his heart and pursue a career in philosophy, and gave him the financial freedom to do so. Still, Arthur had worshipped his father, and mourned him deeply. He must have been relieved by his father's death even while horrified by it, and guilt stricken by his own relief. Furthermore, he seems to have blamed his mother for his father's suicide.[26] It is not surprising that the sensitive young man reacted to all these psychological conflicts by becoming depressed.

Later in life, when Schopenhauer was in his mid-thirties and living in Munich, he suffered another bout with serious depression. One cause of this episode was his distress at the fact that his major works had been published but received little or no attention from the philosophical community.[27] Still later, in his forties, aging and still unrecognized by the philosophical public, living in Berlin, Schopenhauer became deeply depressed again. He was obsessed by loneliness and fear of death, and rarely left his apartment for an entire year.[28] So, the evidence supports the claim that Schopenhauer had a dysthymic personality (if we must use contemporary jargon), and as is typical of such people, he fell into serious, clinical depression at times of major life stress.

What events and conditions in Schopenhauer's life might have contributed to his dysthymia and depression? We can see from Schopenhauer's biography that he grew up desperate to win the love

24. Depression runs in families!
25. Safranski, *Schopenhauer*, p. 56.
26. Safranski, *Schopenhauer*, pp. 54–55.
27. Safranski, *Schopenhauer*, p. 274.
28. Safranski, *Schopenhauer*, p. 280.

of a distant, unhappy father. Meanwhile, his mother treated him rather as an inconvenience; she would have preferred the life of a novelist and socialite, without the bother of children. Schopenhauer never felt secure in his family's (or anybody else's) love. He had a deep fear of abandonment. In his memoirs, he wrote of himself as a child of six: "My parents, returning from a walk one evening, found me in deep despair because suddenly I thought I had been abandoned by them forever."[29] This same fear of abandonment caused him, later in life, to avoid close attachments. (This is classic self-defeating behavior: "If I never allow anyone to get close to me, no one can ever abandon me." It effectively results in the person failing to obtain what he most wants—love.) So, it is fairly clear that Schopenhauer was psychologically conflicted, lonely, and often depressed. But so what? Is a depressive person any less likely to produce true philosophy than a nondepressive person?

Of course, we must note that when one is in the throes of serious, major depression, one cannot think clearly. One's thoughts move as slowly as molasses in January, and one cannot concentrate on anything. Even minor depression can cause the sufferer to find conversation and critical thought painful; hence, he becomes dogmatic and closed-minded. Schopenhauer sometimes suffered from these flaws. Fortunately, however, depression-prone people are not always and constantly in these low states. When able to think clearly (when the illness is in remission, so to speak), depressive people are able to see the world as clearly as anybody else.

It is sometimes tempting to think that depressed (or at least depression-prone) people see the world more clearly than optimists do. I have had this thought. It has sometimes seemed to me that depression is the "disease" of seeing the world too clearly, and that being depressive is a sign of intelligence.[30] On sober reflection, however, I must reject such a view. It is a bad-faith way of flattering myself for being depressive. It is excessively egoistic, a self-serving myth propagated by the gloomy.

As previously noted, it seems likely that many of those who adopt pessimism as a philosophical position do so at least in part because

29. Safranski, *Schopenhauer*, p. 60.

30. This thought has evidently been recurrent in history. Foucault quotes the sixteenth-century writer Thomas Sydenham as saying, "[Melancholics] are people who, apart from their complaint, are prudent and sensible, and who have an extraordinary penetration and sagacity. Thus Aristotle rightly observed that melancholics have more intelligence than other men" (*Madness and Civilization*, p. 118). (For the record, I can't find any such remark in Aristotle's works.)

of personal experience of the living hell that is major depressive illness. There is a curious circularity in all this. It is both the unpleasant nature of the events that lead to depression and the excruciating mental pain of the depression itself that lead one to adopt a pessimistic view of life. I suspect this was true of Schopenhauer.

Salvation as Recovery from Depression

When one has been seriously depressed, one knows why *salvation* is necessary. Indeed, what could salvation be, other than deliverance from that state?

Many of us have had the experience of spending years of our lives in dissatisfaction, frustration, and unhappiness, whether or not our condition is diagnosed as clinical depression. Relief from this condition may come not from any dramatic event, but from a gradual adjustment to, and acceptance of, the basic facts defining one's life, including one's own past choices. One stops trying to run away, realizing there is no better place to which to run. One accepts, "This is my life; this is who I am," and begins to do one's best at the task at hand, instead of bitterly wishing for a different life. One discovers that happiness comes from honoring and respecting one's own character. One begins to spend more time doing what one really enjoys. One's opinions gradually solidify. One begins to say what one really believes, without caring greatly what other people might think. At a certain point, it seems that the world has transformed. It is natural to refer to such a transformation as a kind of "salvation."

Of course, since I am a realist, I must take "the world has transformed" to be merely a colorful metaphor. The world does not really change—the self changes. For Schopenhauer and Wittgenstein, however, it is literally true that the world transforms when the subject, the limit of the world, undergoes a profound change of attitude.

My favorite passage from the *Tractatus* is 6.43: "If the good or bad exercise of the will does alter the world, it can alter only the limits of the world, not the facts—not what can be expressed by means of language. In short, the effect must be that it becomes an altogether different world. It must, so to speak, wax and wane as a whole. The world of the happy man is a different one from that of the unhappy man."[31]

31. Wittgenstein, *Tractatus Logico-Philosophicus*, trans. D. F. Pears and B. F. McGuinness (London: Routledge, 1961), p. 72.

My reflections on the difficulty of separating realism and anti-realism have caused me to doubt whether there is really any difference between a transformation of the soul and a transformation of the world in which the soul dwells.

Many years after his Tractarian phase, Wittgenstein recorded the following remark: "If life becomes hard to bear, we think of a change in our circumstances. But the most important and effective change, a change in our own attitude, hardly ever occurs to us, and the resolution to take such a step is very difficult for us."[32]

Wittgenstein's remark calls our attention again to the attribution fallacy: when life is hard, and we become depressed, we think of a change in our circumstances, assuming that the depression is caused by our circumstances. It is hard for us to entertain the possibility that our circumstances might seem worse than they are because we are depressed, or that our depressive behavior might be making the situation worse than it would otherwise be.

It would be simplistic, however, to conclude that it is always an instance of the attribution fallacy when we say, "My situation is making me depressed." Often, situations *do* make us depressed, and we need to change those situations. It is an immensely difficult matter to figure out how much of our depression is due to the world and how much is due to our own attitude. This is very like the problem in epistemology of trying to distinguish which elements of knowledge come from the world and which elements are supplied by the mind. Perhaps this is what Schopenhauer meant when he said that the solution to the riddle of the world is to be found at the meeting point between inner and outer experience.

The sort of shift in inner attitude we have been discussing is, pretty clearly, not wholly voluntary. When it happens, it seems to come as an unexpected gift. One is not entitled to congratulate oneself on the achievement, because it wasn't anything one *did*. It was something that just *happened*. This may be why some religious traditions have attributed "salvation" to the grace of God rather than to the alleged free will of human beings.

Parker J. Palmer relates an anecdote relevant here. Palmer has suffered from major depression, and overcome it. He writes:

> I once met a woman who had wrestled with depression for most of her adult life. Toward the end of a long and searching conversation…she

---

32. See Wittgenstein, *Culture and Value*, trans. Peter Winch, ed. G. H. Von Wright (Chicago: University of Chicago Press, 1980), p. 53e. This remark dates from 1946.

asked, in a voice full of misery, "Why do some people kill themselves yet others get well?" I knew that her question came from her own struggle to stay alive, so I wanted to answer with care. But I could come up with only one response: "I have no idea. I really have no idea."[33]

Palmer's honesty is moving and refreshing. The "culture of therapy" in which we live tries to make us believe that our mental well-being is completely under our voluntary control, but it is not. There are mysteries here.

One truth I must not neglect to mention is this: depressive people tend to have relapses. Even someone who has undergone a positive shift in inner attitude, accepted herself and the unchangeable conditions of her life, begun to live more gratefully and positively, and so on, will probably experience further problems with depression. Salvation (if you want to call it that) is not a permanent deliverance into peace and tranquility. To be alive is to face trouble and to have moods and reactions. A person who has undergone the sort of significant attitude adjustment we have been discussing is not permanently out of danger; he or she is, however, better equipped to deal with the remainder of life.

Schopenhauer on the "Acquired Character"

Schopenhauer, with his huge ego, craved recognition and praise above all else. He became really happy only as an older man, when people finally started to read and appreciate his work. During his younger years, while he lived in lonely obscurity and struggled with depression, his work was his therapy and his salvation. The creative self-expression of writing his philosophy, not any denial of the will, was what saved him.

So, it is rather curious that Schopenhauer teaches denial of the will as the way to salvation, instead of agreeing with his worthy successor, Jung, that self-realization is the way to salvation.

Schopenhauer comes closest to recognizing the value of self-realization in a section where he discusses "acquired character."[34] Recall that Schopenhauer endorses a distinction between the "intelligible character" (the noumenal aspect of the self, outside space and

---

33. Parker J. Palmer, *Let Your Life Speak: Listening for the Voice of Vocation* (San Francisco: Jossey-Bass, 2000), p. 59.

34. See *WWR*, vol. 1, pp. 301–307.

time) and the "empirical character" (the self as it manifests itself through action determined by motive in the phenomenal world). He holds that we become familiar with our own empirical character only through experience: we find out who we are by watching ourselves over the years and observing our own feelings and actions. Even though we may come to the philosophical realization of the truth of determinism, it would be a mistake to confuse determinism with fatalism and fall into the "lazy man's argument," concluding that we ought not to try to accomplish goals and to improve ourselves, since "what's going to happen is already determined anyway." Crucially, at any given point in time, we *don't know* what we are going to do; we *don't know* what potential may lie in our character.[35] Hence, trying to be our best self is not precluded by determinism and is, so to speak, built into the deterministic plan. The illusion of an open future, caused by our temporal bondedness and our ignorance of ourselves and the world, is necessary in order for us to discover who we really are and what we can really do.[36]

A person does not know who she is until she has lived awhile. She sees that others can do X, Y, and Z, and these activities look rewarding and attractive, so she tries them. This is, in large part, how she spends her youth—trying on identities and finding out what does and does not fit. She may discover that she can't do X, Y, and Z; these things are not in her nature. For her, they lead only to failure, humiliation, and disappointment. So, she finds other activities, activities that suit her nature, at which she can succeed. Gradually, she leaves off trying to be anybody but herself and becomes comfortable with herself. As Schopenhauer so eloquently puts it:

> For just as a fish is happy only in water, a bird only in the air, and a mole under the earth, so every man is happy only in an atmosphere suitable to him. . . . From lack of moderate insight into all this, many a man will make all kinds of abortive attempts; he will do violence to his character in particulars, and yet on the whole will have to yield to it again. What he thus laboriously attains contrary to his nature will give him no pleasure; what he learns in this way will remain dead. . . . We must first learn through experience what we will and what we can do; till then we do not know this, are without [acquired] character, and must often be driven back to our own path

35. See Wittgenstein, *Tractatus*, 5.1362: "The freedom of the will consists in the impossibility of knowing actions that still lie in the future."
36. *WWR*, vol. I, p. 302.

by hard blows from outside. But if we have finally learnt it, we have then obtained what in the world is called character, the *acquired character* which, accordingly, is nothing but the most complete possible knowledge of our own individuality.[37]

I don't know about you, dear reader, but this certainly describes my own path through life! What Schopenhauer says in this context is so good, I must quote him at length:

> Now we shall no longer, as novices, wait, attempt, and grope about, in order to see what we really desire and are able to do; we know this once for all [*sic*].... We know our will in general.... We also know the nature and measure of our powers and weaknesses, and shall thus spare ourselves much pain and suffering. For there is really no other pleasure than in the use and feeling of our own powers, and the greatest pain is when we are aware of a deficiency in our powers where they are needed. Now if we have found out where our strong and weak points lie, we shall attempt to develop, employ, and use in every way those talents that are naturally prominent in us. We shall always turn to where these talents are useful and of value, and shall avoid entirely and with self-restraint those pursuits for which we have little natural aptitude.[38]

There are persons who suffer from chronic depression during their youth and finally are delivered from such depression by this process of developing one's "acquired character." Indeed, developing one's acquired character seems inseparable from the kind of significant attitude adjustment discussed above. I must ask, as I asked in the earlier context: Is this not a kind of *salvation*? After all, it ends a certain kind of deep suffering and misery and brings about, as Schopenhauer himself admits, the greatest possible contentment:

> We are like entrapped elephants, which rage and struggle fearfully for many days, until they see that it is fruitless, and then suddenly offer their necks calmly to the yoke, trained for ever.... If we have clearly recognized once for all [*sic*] our good qualities and strong points as well as our defects and weaknesses; if we have fixed our aim accordingly, and rest content about the unattainable, we thus escape in the surest way, as far as our individuality allows, that bitterest of all sufferings, dissatisfaction with ourselves, which is the inevitable consequence of ignorance of our own individuality.[39]

37. *WWR*, vol. 1, pp. 304–305.
38. *WWR*, vol. 1, p. 305.
39. *WWR*, vol. 1, pp. 306–307.

However, as the just-quoted paragraph implies, Schopenhauer thinks there is a greater and higher kind of salvation, involving abandoning one's individuality rather than embracing it.

Salvation as Denial of the Will

Schopenhauer agrees with Buddhism and Hinduism that extinguishing the ego altogether is the highest ethical goal. The first step on the road to such salvation is to realize that life is essentially and necessarily characterized by suffering. One then comes to the mystical realization of the sameness of the inner nature of all things and feels the suffering of all creation as one's own. This knowledge manifests itself in truly ethical behavior, motivated by compassion. It also manifests itself in asceticism, including sexual celibacy, because one does not want either to encourage one's own painful desires, or to perpetuate the endless cycle of suffering by producing offspring.[40]

Judaism, in the Old Testament, represents life as good ("and God saw that it was good"). Judaism also encourages its people to celebrate sexuality and to "be fruitful and multiply."

Judaism is a life-affirming religion, and, according to Schopenhauer, this indicates that Judaism is *not* one of the deeper religions. Christianity improves upon Judaism by bringing in the realization that life is actually *not* good, but is essentially suffering. This is why its symbol is the cross, a device of torture and execution. True Christianity also teaches that the highest ethical way is celibacy.[41] Those who have tried to transform Christianity into a life-affirming religion (most Protestants, for example) have misunderstood and bastardized it. In its essence, Christianity is a life-denying religion and bears deep affinities with Eastern thought.[42]

Schopenhauer finds many elements in Christianity that disguise, under confusing layers of myth, truths more clearly expressed in Hinduism and Buddhism. The doctrines of "original sin" and "total depravity" represent the truth that by existing at all, we are doomed to participate in the cycle of suffering, destruction, and death.[43] The

---

40. *WWR*, vol. 1, pp. 375–382.

41. See *WWR*, vol. 2, p. 617, where Schopenhauer makes us see the origin of the custom of a bride tossing away her wreath or bouquet. She is actually signaling, "I hereby give up the crown of blessedness."

42. *WWR*, vol. 2, pp. 616–636.

43. *WWR*, vol. 1, p. 355; vol. 2, pp. 603–605.

teachings of a "last judgment" and divine punishment represent the truth that a kind of eternal justice does operate in the universe— since we are all manifestations of a single Will, tormentor and tormented are one; in harming others, we ultimately harm ourselves. The same truth, Schopenhauer thinks, is disguised in the East by the myth of reincarnation.[44]

The sage who is moved by his insights to adopt asceticism might go further and actually torture himself, with fasting, self-castigation, and so forth. Schopenhauer notes that such behavior is typical of saints and enlightened ones in all religious traditions. The sage inflicts pain and deprivation on himself "in order that, by constant privation and suffering, he may more and more break down and kill the will that he recognizes and abhors as the source of his own suffering existence and of the world's."[45]

Such behavior is apparently self-defeating. How does one extinguish suffering by making oneself suffer *more*? (Is there a psychoanalytical explanation for this?) Nevertheless, Schopenhauer correctly says that we can observe saints and mystics from all religions doing the same thing, "mortifying the flesh." This behavior, he says, is an inarticulate way of expressing the intuitive conviction that our will (our desire for comfort, contentment, and happiness) is itself paradoxically the source of all *un*happiness.

The sage also "turns the other cheek" and does not resist when others wrong him:

> [T]he wickedness of others is welcome to him; every injury, every ignominy, every outrage. He gladly accepts them as the opportunity for giving himself the certainty that he no longer affirms the will.... [H]e therefore endures such ignominy and suffering with inexhaustible patience and gentleness, returns good for all evil without ostentation, and allows the fire of anger to rise again within him as little as he does the fire of desires.... [I]f death comes...it is most welcome, and is cheerfully accepted as a longed-for deliverance.[46]

Perhaps such persons exist. The Gospels depict Jesus as such a person, and there are other examples painted for us in literature,[47] but I

---

44. *WWR*, vol. 1, pp. 355–356, 365; vol. 2, pp. 502–504, 603–605.

45. *WWR*, vol. 1, p. 382.

46. *WWR*, vol. 1, p. 382. Schopenhauer talks the talk, but he doesn't walk the walk. Look at how he abuses Hegel!

47. Two who come to mind are Father Zossima in Fyodor Dostoyevsky's *The Brothers Karamazov*, and the Mother Superior in W. Somerset Maugham's *The Painted Veil*.

have never met one. Schopenhauer notes that while such people as St. Francis, the Buddha, and even Spinoza can serve as examples of enlightenment, most of those who reach this state are unknown to history; they live and die in obscurity, with their holiness showing itself only in their "quiet and unobserved conduct."[48]

Schopenhauer's description of such persons is memorable:

[H]ow blessed must be the life of a man whose will is silenced, not for a few moments, as in the enjoyment of the beautiful, but for ever, indeed completely extinguished, except for the last glimmering spark that maintains the body and is extinguished with it. Such a man...is then left only as pure knowing being, as the undimmed mirror of the world. Nothing can distress or alarm him any more; nothing can any longer move him; for he has cut all the thousand threads of willing which hold us bound to the world, and which as craving, fear, envy, and anger drag us here and there in constant pain. He now looks back calmly and with a smile on the phantasmagoria of this world.[49]

In overcoming *will*, the enlightened one subverts his own essence. This ought not to be possible, but it is. This paradox is at the very heart of Schopenhauer's philosophy. As previously noted, Schopenhauer thinks aesthetic experience offers a glimpse, a momentary flash, of this exalted state where the will is left behind—the "peace that passeth all understanding." Schopenhauer states that in the sage who reaches enlightenment, this state of will-less-ness becomes permanent; then he qualifies that view as follows: "[W]e must not imagine that, after the denial of the will-to-live has once appeared through knowledge that has become a quieter of the will, such denial no longer wavers or falters, and that we can rest on it as on an inherited property. On the contrary, it must always be achieved afresh by constant struggle....[O]n earth no one can have lasting peace."[50]

This is maddeningly inconsistent. Does the sage spend the remainder of his life in a state of peace, or does he continue to struggle, and experience only moments of enlightenment? Schopenhauer seems to say both at the same time, and the reader does not know what to make of it. In keeping with what I said earlier about deliverance from depression, I must say that I believe any sort of salvation must

48. *WWR*, vol. 1, pp. 384–386.
49. *WWR*, vol. 1, p. 390.
50. *WWR*, vol. 1, p. 391.

be "achieved afresh by constant struggle." Schopenhauer's more circumspect remarks, as usual, are the more correct ones.

At any rate, Schopenhauer tells us that when the will is denied, the sage *becomes nothing*, without actually dying. In ceasing to will, in ceasing to be individual, he has overcome (or nearly overcome) the "original sin" of existence. It is also possible to see this event conversely: at the moment of enlightenment, the world, with all its suffering and pain, becomes nothing.[51]

One cannot *will* oneself to be a saint. Enlightenment is the result not of will, but of a kind of knowledge that either arrives or doesn't. When it does arrive, this knowledge consumes the will and destroys it. This final bit of knowledge cannot be expressed in words. It comes in silence, and beyond it is only more silence, along with the conduct that expresses (shows) the truth without articulating it. Thus, "all religions at their highest point end in mysticism and mysteries."[52]

Schopenhauer's philosophy, he repeatedly tells us, is a sustained attempt to communicate a "single thought." When one finally understands Schopenhauer, one realizes that the "single thought" cannot be expressed. Schopenhauer faces the same dilemma encountered by Wittgenstein at the end of the *Tractatus*: his book itself, according to itself, cannot say what it means. It can serve only as a ladder that must be thrown away once one has climbed up it.

Now That My Ladder's Gone

First, I must apologize to Yeats for stealing his line to title this final section.[53] However, since I have now put *The World as Will and Representation* aside, after reading it twice (as Schopenhauer himself instructs his readers to do), I think the title is appropriate. Though it is difficult to see how one can evaluate an inexpressible idea, I am going to try to evaluate Schopenhauer's "one thought," and I can

51. *WWR*, vol. 1, p. 412. See also vol. 2, p. 487, p. 507.

52. *WWR*, vol. 2, p. 610.

53. In W. B. Yeats's poem "The Circus Animals' Desertion," he writes of the sad and frustrating mental condition of feeling creatively empty. No poems would come, and he felt used up, able only to repeat old themes, unable to come up with anything new. He closes the poem, "Now that my ladder's gone, I must lie down where all the ladders start, in the foul rag-and-bone shop of the heart."

only do so in the foul rag-and-bone shop of my own reflections on my own experience.

What do I think of all this business about enlightenment as denial of the will? Well, as just indicated, I am happy to admit that persons might exist who have reached the kind of state Schopenhauer describes. If I ever met such people, I would be in awe of them, but they would be incomprehensible to me. The only kind of salvation I know anything about is deliverance from depression by facing the world as it is, accepting it, and accepting oneself. I understand Schopenhauer's "single thought" insofar as it is an intuition of the sameness of the inner nature of all things. I do not understand how it is possible for anyone, or anything, to transcend this nature altogether.

What do I think about pessimism? I am certainly a pessimist. I am inclined to think that there is no ultimate hope, either for any of us as individuals or for the human race as a whole. Everything ends, and ends badly. Though these are my convictions, I agree with the existentialists[54] that such convictions are no excuse to stop trying. Though we may be convinced that the forces of evil will triumph in the end, our lives gain meaning if we continue, anyway, to fight for the true and the good.[55] We do this most effectively by discovering and utilizing our peculiarly individual gifts and talents.[56]

---

54. See, e.g., Albert Camus, *The Myth of Sisyphus* (New York: Random House, 1955). Camus says that hope is the worst sin. Authentic life can begin only when one has given up hope. I understand this, and I agree with it. Similarly, Nietzsche, in discussing the "heroic man" of which he takes Schopenhauer to be a prime example, says, "The heroic man does not think of his happiness or misery, his virtues or his vices, or of his being the measure of things; he has no further hopes of himself and will accept the utter consequences of his hopelessness…the man who looks for a lie in everything, and becomes a willing friend to unhappiness, shall have a marvelous disillusioning: there hovers near him something unutterable, of which truth and happiness are but idolatrous images born of the night; the earth loses her dragging weight, the events and powers of earth become as a dream, and gradual clearness widens round him like a summer evening. It is as though the beholder of these things began to wake, and it had only been the clouds of a passing dream that had been weaving about him. They will at some time disappear: and then will it be day." Nietzsche, *Schopenhauer as Educator*, trans. Adrian Collins, in Oscar Levy, ed., *The Complete Works of Friedrich Nietzsche*, vol. 5 (Edinburgh: Foulis, 1910), pp. 146–147.

55. I have been told that, according to Norse mythology, it is predestined that the forces of evil and darkness will win. Still, it is an honor for a warrior to go down fighting for goodness and light. If this is true, I salute Norse mythology for its profundity.

56. Here again, I agree with Parker J. Palmer. See his *Let Your Life Speak*.

My own view about the nature of salvation connects importantly with this point. Salvation comes, I believe (one is delivered from despair), when one decides to go on and live anyway and do what one can, despite the fact that life is terrible and there is no ultimate hope.[57]

Schopenhauer found life unbearable, until he saved himself through his work. His work is the expression of his nature, of his own brilliant and conflicted soul. Thus, if we look at Schopenhauer's life, instead of listening to his official teaching, we see that Schopenhauer *shows* a path to salvation more accessible to most of us than saintly denial of the will. He shows us that we save ourselves by becoming, and expressing, who we are. We can do this, and find joy in doing it, even in this "worst of all possible worlds."[58]

57. Nietzsche notes that Schopenhauer's philosophy, though pessimistic, radiates "a joy that really makes others joyful." This joy stems from the fact that Schopenhauer conquered the personal demons that plagued him: "[I]t is this that brings the deepest and intensest [sic] joy, to see the conquering god with all the monsters he has fought." *Schopenhauer as Educator*, p. 116. It is interesting that Nietzsche also uses the image of the ladder, describing one's educators as steps on a ladder leading one upward to one's true self. The true self, rather than being deep inside, is "an infinite height above" what one usually takes for oneself. *Schopenhauer as Educator*, p. 107.

58. See *WWR*, vol. 2, p. 583, where Schopenhauer says, "[A]gainst the palpably sophistical proofs of Leibniz that this is the best of all possible worlds, we may even oppose seriously and honestly the proof that it is the *worst* of all possible worlds."

BIBLIOGRAPHY

Allen, Woody. *Match Point* (film). DreamWorks Pictures, 2005.

American Psychiatric Association. *Diagnostic and Statistical Manual of Mental Disorders*, fourth edition, text revision. Washington, D.C.: American Psychiatric Association, 2000.

Ariew, Roger, and Watkins, Eric, eds. *Modern Philosophy: An Anthology of Primary Sources*. Indianapolis: Hackett, 1998.

Aristotle. *Physics, On Generation and Corruption, On the Heavens, Parts of Animals, Metaphysics, De Anima, Nicomachean Ethics*. Selections reprinted in S. Marc Cohen, Patricia Curd, and C. D. C. Reeve, eds., *Readings in Ancient Philosophy*. Indianapolis: Hackett, 1995, pp. 522–719.

Atwell, John E. *Schopenhauer: The Human Character*. Philadelphia: Temple University Press, 1990.

Atwell, John E. *Schopenhauer on the Character of the World: The Metaphysics of Will*. Berkeley: University of California Press, 1995.

Austin, J. L. *Sense and Sensibilia*. Selections reprinted in Michael Huemer, ed., *Epistemology: Contemporary Readings*. London: Routledge, 2002, pp. 74–83.

Benatar, David. *Better Never to Have Been: The Harm of Coming into Existence*. Oxford: Oxford University Press, 2006.

Berkeley, George. *Principles of Human Knowledge*, Part I. In Roger Ariew and Eric Watkins, eds., *Modern Philosophy: An Anthology of Primary Sources*. Indianapolis: Hackett, 1998, pp. 470–477.

Brockhaus, Richard R. *Pulling Up the Ladder: The Metaphysical Roots of Wittgenstein's Tractatus Logico-Philosophicus*. La Salle, Ill.: Open Court, 1991.

Camus, Albert. *The Myth of Sisyphus*. New York: Random House, 1955.

Clayton, Philip. *Mind and Emergence*. Oxford: Oxford University Press, 2004.

Cushing, James T. *Philosophical Concepts in Physics: The Historical Relation between Philosophy and Scientific Theories*. Cambridge: Cambridge University Press, 1998.

Davidson, Donald. "Mental Events." In Davidson, *Essays on Actions and Events*. Oxford: Clarendon Press, 1980, pp. 207–227.

Davidson, Donald. "Thought and Talk." In Davidson, *Inquiries into Truth and Interpretation*. Oxford: Clarendon Press, 1984, pp. 155–170.

Davies, Paul. *The 5th Miracle: The Search for the Origin and Meaning of Life*. New York: Simon and Schuster, 1999.

Descartes, René. *Meditations on First Philosophy*, translated by Donald A. Cress. Indianapolis: Hackett, 1993.

DeWitt, Richard. *Worldviews: An Introduction to the History and Philosophy of Science*. Oxford: Blackwell, 2004.

Dostoyevsky, Fyodor. *The Brothers Karamazov*. New York: New American Library, 1957.

Dretske, Fred. *Explaining Behavior: Reasons in a World of Causes*. Cambridge: MIT Press, 1988.

Dummett, Michael. *The Logical Basis of Metaphysics*. London: Duckworth, 1991.

Feldman, Fred. "An Examination of Kantian Ethics." In Louis P. Pojman, ed., *Moral Philosophy: A Reader*, third edition. Indianapolis: Hackett, 2003, pp. 214–228.

Foucault, Michel. *Madness and Civilization: A History of Insanity in the Age of Reason*, translated by Richard Howard. New York: Random House, 1965.

Foucault, Michel. *The Birth of the Clinic: An Archaeology of Medical Perception*, translated by A. M. Sheridan Smith. New York: Random House, 1973.

Freud, Sigmund. *An Outline of Psycho-analysis*, translated by James Strachey. New York: W. W. Norton and Co., 1949.

Freud, Sigmund. *Civilization and Its Discontents*, translated by James Strachey. New York: W. W. Norton and Co., 1961.

Griffin, James. *Wittgenstein's Logical Atomism*. Oxford: Clarendon Press, 1964.

Hacking, Ian. *Re-writing the Soul: Multiple Personality and the Sciences of Memory*. Princeton: Princeton University Press, 1995.

Hacking, Ian. *The Social Construction of What?* Cambridge: Harvard University Press, 1999.

Heil, John. *From an Ontological Point of View*. Oxford: Oxford University Press, 2003.

Heisenberg, Werner. *Physics and Philosophy: The Revolution in Modern Science*. Amherst, N.Y.: Prometheus Books, 1999.

Herbert, Nick. *Quantum Reality: Beyond the New Physics*. New York: Doubleday, 1985.

Honderich, Ted. *How Free Are You? The Determinism Problem*. Oxford: Oxford University Press, 1993.

Hume, David. *A Treatise of Human Nature*, edited by Ernest C. Mossner. Baltimore: Penguin, 1969.

James, William. *The Varieties of Religious Experience*. New York: New American Library, 1958.

Janaway, Christopher. *Self and World in Schopenhauer's Philosophy*. Oxford: Oxford University Press, 1989.

Janaway, Christopher. *Schopenhauer*. Oxford: Oxford University Press, 1994.

Janaway, Christopher. "Will and Nature." In Janaway, ed., *The Cambridge Companion to Schopenhauer*. Cambridge: Cambridge University Press, 1999.

Janik, Allan, and Toulmin, Stephen. *Wittgenstein's Vienna*. New York: Simon and Schuster, 1973.

Jeans, Sir James. *Physics and Philosophy*. New York: Dover, 1981.

Jung, Carl Gustav. *The Essential Jung*, edited and introduced by Anthony Storr. Princeton: Princeton University Press, 1983.

Kahane, Howard. "Sociobiology, Egoism, and Reciprocity." In Louis P. Pojman, ed., *Moral Philosophy: A Reader*, third edition. Indianapolis: Hackett, 2003, pp. 87–103.

Kant, Immanuel. *Foundations of the Metaphysics of Morals*, translated by Lewis White Beck. Indianapolis: Bobbs-Merrill, 1959.

Kant, Immanuel. *Critique of Pure Reason*, translated by Norman Kemp Smith. New York: St. Martin's, 1965.

Kant, Immanuel. *Prolegomena to Any Future Metaphysics*, translated by James W. Ellington. Indianapolis: Hackett, 1977.

Kant, Immanuel. *Critique of Practical Reason*, translated by Lewis White Beck. Upper Saddle River, N.J.: Prentice-Hall, 1993.

Kim, Jaegwon. "The Non-reductivists' Troubles with Mental Causation." In John Heil and Alfred Mele, eds., *Mental Causation*. Oxford: Oxford University Press, 1993, pp. 189–210.

Kuhn, Thomas S. *The Essential Tension: Selected Studies in Scientific Tradition and Change*. Chicago: University of Chicago Press, 1977.

Leibniz, G. W. *Discourse on Metaphysics* and *Monadology*. Reprinted in Daniel Garber and Roger Ariew, eds., *Discourse on Metaphysics and Other Essays*. Indianapolis: Hackett, 1991, pp. 1–41, 68–81.

Leibniz, G. W. Letter to Antoine Arnauld, Nov. 28–Dec. 8, 1686. Excerpts reprinted in Roger Ariew and Eric Watkins, eds., *Modern Philosophy: An Anthology of Primary Sources*. Indianapolis: Hackett, 1998, pp. 214–217.

Lowe, E. J. *Subjects of Experience*. Cambridge: Cambridge University Press, 1996.

Mackie, J. L. *Ethics: Inventing Right and Wrong*. New York: Viking Penguin Books, 1977.

Martin, C. B. *The Mind in Nature*. Oxford: Oxford University Press, 2007.

Maugham, W. Somerset. *The Painted Veil*. New York: Vintage, 2004.

McDowell, John. *Mind and World*. Cambridge: Harvard University Press, 1994.

Mill, John Stuart. *On Liberty*. Indianapolis: Hackett, 1978.

Mill, John Stuart. *Utilitarianism*. Indianapolis: Hackett, 1979.

Molnar, George. *Powers: A Study in Metaphysics*. Oxford: Oxford University Press, 2003.

Monk, Ray. *Ludwig Wittgenstein: The Duty of Genius*. London: Vintage, 1990.

Moore, G. E. "Proof of an External World." Portions reprinted in Michael Huemer, ed., *Epistemology: Contemporary Readings*. London: Routledge, 2002, pp. 602–605.

Nietzsche, Friedrich. *Schopenhauer as Educator*, translated by Adrian Collins. In Oscar Levy, ed., *The Complete Works of Friedrich Nietzsche*, volume 5. Edinburgh: Foulis, 1910.

Pagels, Heinz R. *The Cosmic Code: Quantum Physics as the Language of Nature*. Toronto: Bantam Books, 1982.

Palmer, Parker J. *Let Your Life Speak: Listening for the Voice of Vocation*. San Francisco: Jossey-Bass, 2000.

Pereboom, Derk. *Living without Free Will*. Cambridge: Cambridge University Press, 2001.

Plato. *Republic*. Selections reprinted in S. Marc Cohen, Patricia Curd, and C. D. C. Reeve, eds., *Ancient Greek Philosophy*. Indianapolis: Hackett, 1995, pp. 253–431.

Putnam, Hilary. "Brains in a Vat." In Michael Huemer, ed., *Epistemology: Contemporary Readings*. London: Routledge, 2002, pp. 524–538.

Quine, W. V. O. "Two Dogmas of Empiricism." Reprinted in Michael Huemer, ed., *Epistemology: Contemporary Readings*. London: Routledge, 2002, pp. 176–193.

Quine, W. V. O., and Ullian, J. S. *The Web of Belief*. New York: Random House, 1970.

Reid, Thomas. *Essays on the Intellectual Powers of Man*. Selections reprinted in Michael Huemer, ed., *Epistemology: Contemporary Readings*. London: Routledge, 2002, pp. 51–63.

Ross, W. D. *The Right and the Good* (Oxford, 1930). Selections reprinted in Louis P. Pojman, ed., *Moral Philosophy: A Reader*, third edition. Indianapolis: Hackett, 2003, pp. 229–238.

Russell, Bertrand. *The Autobiography of Bertrand Russell, 1872–1914*. Boston: Little-Brown, 1967.

Russell, Bertrand. *The Problems of Philosophy*. Buffalo: Prometheus Books, 1988.

Safranski, Rudiger. *Schopenhauer and the Wild Years of Philosophy*, translated by Ewald Osers. Cambridge: Harvard University Press, 1989.

Schopenhauer, Arthur. *The World as Will and Representation*, volumes 1 and 2, translated by E. F. J. Payne. New York: Dover, 1969.

Schopenhauer, Arthur. *On the Fourfold Root of the Principle of Sufficient Reason*, translated by E. F. J. Payne. La Salle, Ill.: Open Court, 1974.

Schopenhauer, Arthur. *On the Will in Nature*, translated by E. F. J. Payne; introduction by David E. Cartwright. New York: Berg, 1992.

Schopenhauer, Arthur. *On the Basis of Morality*, translated by E. F. J. Payne; introduction by David E. Cartwright. Indianapolis: Hackett, 1995.

Schopenhauer, Arthur. *Prize Essay on the Freedom of the Will*, translated by E. F. J. Payne; edited by Gunter Zoller. Cambridge: Cambridge University Press, 1999.

Sellars, Wilfrid. *Empiricism and the Philosophy of Mind*. Cambridge: Harvard University Press, 1997.

Shoemaker, Sydney. "Causality and Properties." Reprinted in Tim Crane and Katalin Farkas, eds., *Metaphysics: A Guide and Anthology*. Oxford: Oxford University Press, 2006, pp. 273–295.

Sosa, Ernest, and Tooley, Michael, eds. *Causation*. Oxford: Oxford University Press, 1993.

Spinoza, Benedict de. *Ethics*, translated by R. H. M. Elwes. New York: Dover, 1955.

Sulloway, Frank J. *Freud: Biologist of the Mind*. Cambridge: Harvard University Press, 1992.

Toulmin, Stephen, and Janik, Allan. *Wittgenstein's Vienna*. New York: Simon and Schuster, 1973.

Wittgenstein, Ludwig. *Tractatus Logico-Philosophicus*, translated by C. K. Ogden, with original German on facing pages. London: Routledge and Kegan Paul, 1922.

Wittgenstein, Ludwig. *Philosophical Investigations*, translated by G. E. M. Anscombe. New York: Macmillan, 1953.

Wittgenstein, Ludwig. *Tractatus Logico-Philosophicus*, translated by D. F. Pears and B. F. McGuinness. London: Routledge and Kegan Paul, 1961.

Wittgenstein, Ludwig. *Culture and Value*, translated by Peter Winch; edited by G. H. Von Wright. Chicago: University of Chicago Press, 1980.

Wittgenstein, Ludwig. "Lecture on Ethics." In *Ludwig Wittgenstein: Philosophical Occasions 1912–1951*, edited by James Klagge and Alfred Nordmann. Indianapolis: Hackett, 1993, pp. 37–44.

Yeats, W. B. "The Circus Animals' Desertion." In *The Collected Poems of W. B. Yeats*, edited by Richard J. Finnerman. New York: Macmillan, 1989, pp. 346–348.

Young, Julian. *Schopenhauer*. London: Routledge, 2005.

INDEX

acquired character. *See* character,
    acquired
action, 6, 7, 13, 20, 28–31, 42–43,
    52, 55, 59
    autonomous, 52, 59
    as caused by character and
      motive, 20, 28–31
    explanation of, 6, 7
    and Kant's refutation of idealism,
      42, 43
    in Leibniz's metaphysics, 55
    responsibility for, 29–31
    as revealing metaphysical
      convictions, 13
    voluntary, 6, 7
aesthetics, 102–115
agent causation. *See* cause, agent
Alcibiades, 4n2
Allen, Woody, 121n3
altruism, 57
Anderson, Abraham "Brom," 41n11
animal intelligence. *See* animals,
    nonhuman
animals, nonhuman, 5, 7, 10, 19,
    23, 29, 46–47, 82, 104, 113–114
animal spirits, 8

animism, 52, 56. *See also*
    panpsychism
antimoral incentives, 91–92
antinomy, 9–10, 48
anti-realism, 48n28, 49–50, 107,
    119. *See also* idealism
appetition, as activity of Leibniz's
    monads, 55, 61–62
architecture, 102, 104
Aristotle, 15, 53, 55, 61, 74n6,
    132n30
    doctrine of substantial forms of,
      15, 53,55
    ethics of, 74n6 (*see also*
      eudaimonism)
    metaphysical views of, 53, 61
Arnauld, Antoine, 55n37
art, 51, 102, 105, 114–115
    as depicting natural forces,
      114–115
    as quieting the will, 105
    as revealing Platonic forms, 51,
      102, 105
    See also aesthetics
attributes, in Spinoza's metaphysics,
    56, 56n38